A Way with Words
Book 2

UNIVERSITY OF CAMBRIDGE
RESEARCH CENTRE FOR ENGLISH
AND APPLIED LINGUISTICS
KEYNES HOUSE
TRUMPINGTON STREET
CAMBRIDGE CB2 1QA

A Way with Words

Vocabulary development activities
for learners of English

Book 2

*Stuart Redman
and Robert Ellis*

Advisory editor: Michael McCarthy

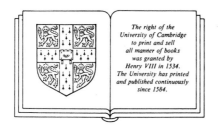

The right of the
University of Cambridge
to print and sell
all manner of books
was granted by
Henry VIII in 1534.
The University has printed
and published continuously
since 1584.

Cambridge University Press
Cambridge
New York   Port Chester
Melbourne   Sydney

Published by the Press Syndicate of the University of Cambridge
The Pitt Building, Trumpington Street, Cambridge CB2 1RP
40 West 20th Street, New York, NY 10011, USA
10 Stamford Road, Oakleigh, Melbourne 3166, Australia

© Cambridge University Press 1990

First published 1990

Printed in Great Britain
by Scotprint Ltd, Musselburgh, Scotland

ISBN 0 521 35919 8 Student's Book
ISBN 0 521 35920 1 Teacher's Book
ISBN 0 521 35027 1 Cassette

GO

Contents

Thanks

We would like to thank the following people:

Our Commissioning Editor, Jeanne McCarten, and Advisory Editor, Michael McCarthy, for their continued support and guidance.

Ruth Gairns, for contributing ideas to the book, and also for her continued support and encouragement.

The teachers at The London School of English, The Bell Language Institute (London), and the many other schools and colleges throughout the world who have piloted the material and given us such important feedback.

And finally Alison Silver, our Desk Editor, for the invaluable contribution she has made to this book, and also the rest of the production team at CUP.

1 Studying vocabulary

1 Organising new words

a When you learn words and phrases, your memory tries to group words that go together so that one word or phrase will remind you of others. Look at the different groupings below on the left, and match each one with the correct example on the right.

1 Related to the same topic
2 Examples of a more general word
3 Similar in meaning
4 Opposite in meaning
5 Arranged along a scale
6 Built from the same basic word
7 Steps in the same process

lazy/hard-working

draw/paint

SUBJECT	letter
mathematics	word
biology	phrase
literature	sentence
geography	paragraph
physics	page
chemistry	chapter
history	book

write	take an exam
writer	pass/fail
unwritten	revise
typewriter	nervous
	a grade

listen to a lecture/take notes
write an essay

Look at the words and phrases in the box below and try to group them in these ways.

drunk	ring	depend
breeze	independent	article
journalist	bracelet	caption
wealthy	release the handbrake	picture
dependable	wind	jewellery
put into gear	necklace	push in the clutch
earrings	headline	editor
sober	well-off	gale
newspaper	look in the mirror	independence

Now compare your answers with a partner and discuss the differences.

b Find or think of a group of words or phrases which you have learnt recently and see if it fits in any of the groups above. Carry on until you find a group of words or phrases which is *not* in the groups above. Ask your partner if he or she agrees.

──── **2** Ways of explaining new words ────

a Complete the crossword below:

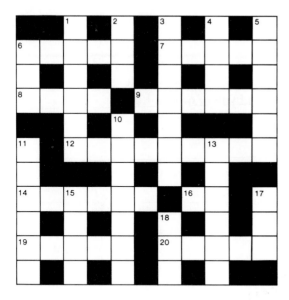

12 What you get at school. (9)
14 The opposite of *defend*. (6)
16 If you don't know the answer you should look it .... in your dictionary. (2)
19 A synonym for *rub out*. (5)
20 A synonym for *mistake*. (5)

DOWN

1 Soldiers may fight one of these in a war. (6)
2 The person who treats sick animals. (3)
3 The opposite of *legal*. (7)
4 The stuff you use for washing yourself. (4)
5 The general word for gun, knife, rifle, etc. (6)
6 It's spelt like *knew* but sounds like *know*. (3)
10 The place where you get meat. (7)
11 They're a kind of fruit. (6)
13 The opposite of *export*. (6)
15 It's pronounced like *fear* and *bear*, and has two different meanings. (4)
17 A type of vehicle. (3)
18 A type of insect. (3)

ACROSS

6 The opposite of *fresh* bread. (5)
7 Often confused with *lose*. (5)
8 I don't get on very well .... my boss. (4)
9 He was running so fast I couldn't .... (4,2)

b Some of the clues in the crossword are common ways of explaining new words and phrases. Write your own examples using the following phrases, and then see if a partner can guess the word or phrase:

It's a synonym for ....
It's the opposite of ....
It's a kind/type of ....
It's the general word for ...., ..., ..., etc.

It's the place where ....
It's the thing/stuff you use for ....ing.
It's a person who ....

c Find some clues/answers in the crossword which are related to the same single topic. Compare your answers with your partner. If you have both found the same topic, find another one together.

——— **3** Recording and remembering words ———

a   Does this happen to you?

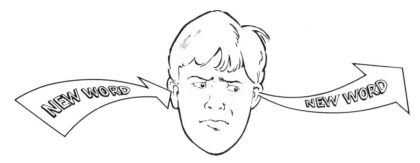

Here is one system that could help you. Work with a partner. One of you must read the following text and then explain it to your partner. Your partner should go straight to **b**.

Peter from Zürich

First of all, I bought myself a box and I got about 250 plain cards to go in it. I also bought four dividers so that I could have five separate sections in the box.

When I learnt a new word or phrase, I wrote it on one side of a card, and on the other side I wrote a German translation and an example sentence in English. I also put whether it was a noun, a verb, or an adjective, etc. The card then went into the first section of the box.

When I had about 30 cards in my box, I started to test myself each evening (never for more than two to three minutes). I looked at one side of the card and tried to remember what was on the other side (English to German and German to English). If I was correct, the card then went into the next section of the box; if I didn't remember, it stayed where it was. When I answered correctly about a word or phrase from the fifth section of the box, I threw that card away because I knew the word.

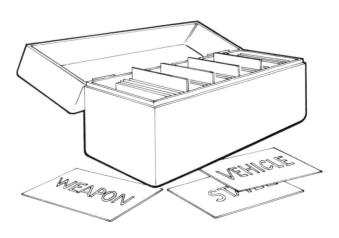

b You need six pieces of paper (approximately 10 cm × 10 cm). Write the following words on your pieces of paper, one word on each piece:

cucumber   solicitor   tools   stapler   melt   blunt

Using a dictionary, find the meaning of each word. On the back of each piece of paper write the following:

1 The part of speech (i.e. noun, verb, etc.).
2 A translation for the word, or a definition in your first language, or a definition in English, or a picture.
3 A short example sentence.

When your partner has explained the text in **a** to you, you must then teach these words to your partner.

c This is one system for remembering new words and phrases. What do you think of it? Can you think of other ways of remembering new vocabulary? Discuss this in groups.

—— 4 All about dictionaries ——————————

a 🔲 Listen to the talk about dictionaries on the cassette and make notes on the different features of dictionaries that are mentioned. When you have finished, compare your notes with your partner.

b Look at the following dictionary entries taken from four different dictionaries. Working with your partner, see how many of the features mentioned in the talk you can find in these entries.

re·fuse¹ /rɪˈfjuːz/ *v* **1** [I;T] to state one's strong unwillingness to accept; say no (to): *He asked her to marry him but she refused.|She refused his offer.* **2** [T+obj(i)+obj(d)] to not give or allow: *We were refused entry|refused permission to enter.* **3** [T+to-v; *obj*] to show or state strong unwillingness (to do something): *She flatly refused to have anything to do with the plan.|The engine refused to start.|I told him to come back but he refused to.|I refuse to answer that question.* ■ USAGE 1 **Refuse, decline, reject,** and **turn down** all mean that you do not do something that you are asked to do (opposite **agree to**), or do not take something that you are offered (opposite **accept**). You can **refuse** or **decline** an invitation; **refuse** permission; **decline, reject,** or **turn down** a suggestion; **refuse, decline, reject,** or **turn down** an offer; **reject** or **turn down** a plan or proposal. 2 **Decline** is more polite than **refuse** and not so firm. Compare *I'm afraid I must decline your invitation/decline to answer that question* and *The prisoner refused to give his name.* 3 You must **decline** in words: *The horse refused* (not **declined**) *to jump the fence.* You need not **reject** or **refuse** something in words: *The horse rejected/refused the apple.*
ref·use² /ˈrefjuːs/ *n* [U] *fml* waste material; RUBBISH: *a heap of kitchen refuse|a refuse dump* (=where a town's waste material is put)

Longman Dictionary of
Contemporary English

re·fuse¹ /ˈrefjuːs/ *n* [U] waste or worthless material; rubbish: *kitchen, garden, household, etc refuse* ○ [attrib] *a refuse bag, dump, bin, etc* ○ *refuse disposal.*
□ **ˈrefuse collector** (*fml*) = DUSTMAN (DUST).
re·fuse² /rɪˈfjuːz/ *v* [I, Tn, Tt, Dn·n] say or show that one is unwilling to give, accept, grant or do sth: *refuse one's consent, help, permission* ○ *refuse a gift, an offer, an invitation* ○ *She refused him/his proposal of marriage.* ○ *Our application for visas was refused.* ○ *The car absolutely refused to start.* ○ *I was refused admittance.* Cf AGREE 1.

Oxford Advanced Learner's
Dictionary of Current English

keen /kiːn/ *adj* **1** [+*to-v*] having a strong, active interest; eager: *a keen student of politics|keen competition for the job|(BrE) keen to pass the examination|She's keen on* (=very interested in) *football/ passing the examination.* **2** (of the mind, the feelings, the five senses, etc.) good, strong, quick at understanding, deeply felt, etc.: *a keen mind|a keen desire|keen sight* **3** sharp; with a fine cutting edge **–keenly** *adv* **–keenness** *n* [U]

*Longman Active Study
Dictionary of English*

feed[1] /fiːd/ *v* (*pt, pp* **fed** /fed/) **1 (a)** [Tn, Tn·pr] ~ **sb/sth (on sth)** give food to (a person or an animal): *She has a large family to feed.* ○ *Have the pigs been fed yet?* ○ *Have you fed the chickens?* ○ *The baby needs feeding.* ○ *The baby can't feed itself yet,* ie can't put food into its own mouth. ○ *What do you feed your dog on?* **(b)** [Dn·n, Dn·pr] ~ **sth to sb/sth** give (a person or an animal) sth as food: *feed the baby some more stewed apple* ○ *feed oats to horses.* **2 (a)** [I, Ipr] ~ **(on sth)** (of animals, or jokingly of humans) eat: *Have you fed yet?* ○ *The cows were feeding on hay in the barn.* **(b)** [Tn] serve as food for (a person or an animal): *There's enough here to feed us all.* **3** [Tn, Tn·pr] ~ **A (with B)/** ~ **B into A** supply (sth) with material; supply (material) to sth: *The lake is fed by several small streams.* ○ *feed the fire (with wood)* ○ *The moving belt feeds the machine with raw material/feeds raw material into the machine.* **4** [Tn] (in football, etc) send passes to (a player). **5** (idm) **bite the hand that feeds one** ⇨ BITE[1]. **6** (phr v) **feed on sth** be nourished or strengthened by sth: *Hatred feeds on envy.* **feed sb up** give extra food to sb to make him more healthy: *You look very pale; I think you need feeding up a bit.* □ **'feeding-bottle** *n* bottle with a rubber teat for feeding liquid foods to young babies or animals. **feed**[2] /fiːd/ *n* **1** [C] meal, usu for animals or babies: *When is the baby's next feed?* **2** [U] **(a)** food for animals: *There isn't enough feed left for the hens.* **(b)** material supplied to a machine. **3** [C] pipe, channel, etc along which material is carried to a machine: *The petrol feed is blocked.*

*Oxford Advanced Learner's
Dictionary of Current English*

keen /kiːn/, **keener, keenest**
   1 Someone who is **keen 1.1** wants to do something very much or wants something to happen very much. ᴇɢ *Her solicitor was much keener to talk to her than she was to talk to him... He's not at all keen for Charlotte or anybody else to know that... I'm never very keen on keeping a car for more than a year.* ◊ **keenness**. ᴇɢ *The only thing I could see in him was a certain keenness for action.* **1.2** has a great deal of enthusiasm for a particular activity, for example a sport or a hobby, and spends a lot of time doing it. ᴇɢ *He was not a keen gardener... Boys are just as keen on cooking as girls are.* **1.3** has an enthusiastic nature and is interested in everything they do. ᴇɢ *...a keen, enthusiastic lad... We should be looking for an abler, keener, more resourceful President.*
   2 A **keen** desire, emotion, or interest is one that is extreme and intense. ᴇɢ *He took a keen interest in domestic affairs... ...a keen desire to see the union brought under the rule of law.* ◊ **keenly**. ᴇɢ *I was still keenly interested in outdoor activities... He felt the pain in his side keenly.*
   3 If you are **keen** on someone, you feel attracted to them and would like to get to know them better; an informal use. ᴇɢ *Molly was very keen on the music master.*

ADJ QUALIT :
PRED, USU +
*to-*INF/*on*
= anxious

◊ N UNCOUNT

ADJ QUALIT : IF +
PREP THEN *on*
= enthusiastic

ADJ QUALIT

ADJ QUALIT : USU
ATTRIB
= deep, intense
◊ ADV WITH VB

ADJ QUALIT :
PRED + *on*

*Collins COBUILD English
Language Dictionary*

feed[1] /fiːd/ *v* **fed** /fed/, **feeding 1** [T *on, with*] to give food to: *to feed the dog on meat, The baby will soon learn to feed himself.* (fig.) *to feed the fire with logs* **2** [I] (esp. of animals or babies) to eat: *The horses were feeding quietly in the field. Cows feed on grass.* **3** [T] to put, supply, or provide, esp. continually: *to feed the wire into/through the hole The information is fed into the company's computer.*
feed[2] *n* **1** [C] a meal taken by an animal or baby **2** [U] food for animals: *a bag of hen feed*

*Longman Active Study
Dictionary of English*

c Now look up the same three words in *your* dictionary. What information does it give you? Is there enough information?

d Discuss with your partner the advantages and disadvantages of a bilingual dictionary compared with a monolingual dictionary.

SELF-STUDY ACTIVITIES

1 Read this sentence and answer the questions below:

> 'No doubt you have read that the knights of the Dark Ages preferred the sword to the plough, travelled everywhere on horseback, and wrote never-ending love letters to their Queen.'

a) How many words are hyphenated?
b) How many words contain a silent letter? (e.g. bom<u>b</u>)
c) How many words are written with a capital letter?
d) How many words are written with a double consonant?

2 In the crossword on page 2, you had an example of a fruit, an insect and a vehicle. How many more examples can you think of for each of these?

FRUIT: ....

INSECTS: ....

VEHICLES: ....

2 Beginnings and endings: Affixation 1

'This one frankly admits it's overpriced!'

You can change the *root* of a word by adding a *prefix* to the beginning of the root, or a *suffix* to its end:

Examples:

eat (v.)	+ over-	=	overeat (i.e. eat too much)
kind (adj.)	+ un-	=	unkind (i.e. not kind)
kind (adj.)	+ -ness	=	kindness (noun)
perform (v.)	+ -ance	=	performance (noun)

These examples show a common feature of prefixes and suffixes, namely that prefixes often change the *meaning* of the word, while suffixes often change the *word class* (i.e. from verb to noun, or noun to adjective, etc.). In this unit we are going to look at some common prefixes and suffixes.

———— 1 ————

a We can make many nouns in the following way:

verb + -ment	e.g. improvement
verb + -tion/sion	e.g. adoption, confusion
verb + -ation/ition	e.g. organisation, proposition
verb + -er/or	e.g. owner, actor

And we can make many adjectives like this:

verb + -ive	e.g. attractive
verb + -ative/itive	e.g. affirmative, sensitive
verb + -able/ible	e.g. readable, convertible

N.B. You will notice there is sometimes a change in spelling. One of the most common changes is to drop the final 'e'.

Examples:
sense – sensitive   organise – organisation

Study the following verbs. How many nouns and adjectives can you form from them using the suffixes above?

predict   invent   enjoy   imagine   adjust   adapt

b Work in groups of three. Can you think of an example of each of these?

1 Something you wear or carry which is adjustable.
2 A film which has been adapted from a book.
3 Something you can never predict accurately.

⟫→

  4 A recent invention which has had a great effect on your life.
  5 An animal or insect which is very adaptable.
  6 A prediction which will almost certainly come true.
  7 A product which is adjustable but should not require adjustment.
  8 An invention which helps some people to wake up and others to go to sleep.
  9 A game which requires imagination but is often very predictable.
 10 Something which one of you finds enjoyable and the others do not.

---- **2** --

a The prefix 're-' can be used with certain verbs, where it often has the meaning *to do something again.*

Example:
I'm going to reread that chapter. = I'm going to read it again.

Write a logical response to the following sentences, including a suitable verb with the prefix 're-'. When you have finished, check in the dictionary to see if your verb exists.

Example:
A: I'm sorry but I can't read your essay.
B: Do you want me to rewrite it?

1 A: They knocked down that house last month.

   B: ....

2 A: My teacher said my homework was terrible.

   B: ....

3 A: That shop's closing down next month.

   B: ....

4 A: What do they do with old bottles and newspapers?

   B: ....

5 A: The department is in a terrible mess – it's so inefficient.

   B: ....

6 A: Two of the prisoners have escaped.

   B: ....

7 A: I failed my exam.

   B: ....

8 A: If I meet you on Tuesday, I won't be able to keep my appointment at the dentist's.

   B: ....

b Can you think of more verbs where you can use the prefix 're-'?

─── 3 ───

a The suffix '-less' often has the meaning *without*, e.g. *a toothless man* is a man without teeth. The opposite meaning is often conveyed with the suffix '-ful', e.g. *careless* and *careful* are opposites. (You must be careful, though. The opposite of *toothless* is NOT *toothful*.)

Which of the following adjectives can form an opposite with '-ful'?

hopeless   endless   tactless   thoughtless   homeless   harmless

b Try to think of a word with '-less' for the following sentences. You will need some words from the list in **a**, but others you will have to guess. Check in a dictionary to see if your word exists and has the correct meaning.

Example:
These people have nowhere to live.   They're ...*homeless*...

1 She makes a lot of silly mistakes in
   her compositions.   She's ....

2 This tin opener doesn't work at all.   It's ....

3 He never thinks about other people.   He's very ....

4 This soup has no flavour at all.   It's ....

5 I had an injection but it didn't hurt.   It was ....

6 That boy is so stupid.   He's ....

7 Don't worry, the dog won't bite you.   It's ....

8 I'm always putting my foot in it.   I'm very ....

─── SELF-STUDY ACTIVITIES ───

1 A number of prefixes can be used with adjectives to give the opposite meaning, e.g. *happy/unhappy, correct/incorrect*. Look back at the adjectives in Exercise **1** of this unit (including the examples). How many of these adjectives form opposites with 'un-' or 'in-'? Check in your dictionary to see if you are right.

2 Find a text (from a coursebook or an English newspaper) and pick out any nouns or adjectives with the suffixes used in Exercise **1** of this unit. Try forming some verbs from these words and then check in a dictionary to see if your verbs exist.

3 The prefix 'un-' is used with certain verbs to mean the opposite action, e.g. *plug in* the TV, *unplug* the TV. Write sentences using 'un-' with the following verbs.

   fasten   pack   do up   wrap up   lock

3 Words around the house

——— 1 ———

a Study the five lists below. What do you think *it* refers to in each case? Write your answers by each letter and then discuss your answers with a partner.

You can . . .

A	B	C	D	E
wash it	lock it	empty it	crack it	wash it
scratch it	break it	lock it	open it	polish it
reverse it	scratch it	open it	empty it	bend it
fix it	fix it	pack it	shake it	sharpen it
dent it	slam it	carry it	fill it	hold it

b You had a lot of accidents in the house today. Which explanation goes with which accident?

1 I broke a plate.
2 I scratched the table.
3 I cracked the glass in one of the windows.
4 I damaged a chair.
5 I stained my shirt.
6 I burnt the carpet.
7 I bent a knife.

8 I dented the cooker.

I was smoking a cigarette and . . .
I was trying to open a bottle with it and . . .
I was fixing the car and . . .

I was drying the dishes and . . .
I dropped a saucepan and . . .
I was standing on it and . . .
I was trying to shut it during the thunderstorm and . . .
I was moving a vase and . . .

c Choose another *it* like the ones in **a**. List five things you can do to it and then see if your partner can guess what *it* is.

——— 2 ———

a Look at the pairs of pictures below. Can you name each of the objects and explain the difference between them?

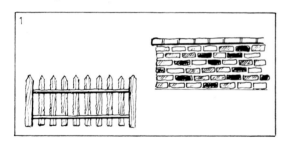

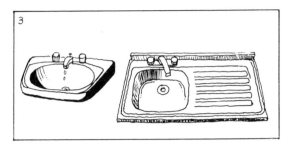

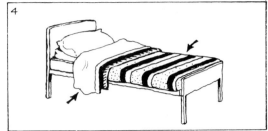

b Check your answers to **a** by listening to the definitions on the cassette.

c Explain the difference between the items in each of the following pairs. Use a dictionary to help you and work with a partner:

floor / ground	ceiling / roof	basement / cellar
flat / apartment	door / gate	

——— 3 ———

a What do you call . . .

The place where you walk in the garden?
The things that grow in the garden?
The place where fish live in the garden?
An insect that buzzes in the garden?
The things that give colour to the garden?
The biggest thing in the garden?
The thing around the garden made of brick?
The wooden thing around the garden?
The way into the garden?
The grass in the garden?
The thing that shines on the garden?
One of the smallest things in the garden?
Where the water comes from in the garden?
What you have to dig in the garden?
A plant you do not want in the garden?
A place where you can sit in the garden?

```
F  E  N  C  E  E  B
L  L  A  W  N  U  P
G  P  O  N  D  A  L
S  A  P  W  T  D  A
U  T  T  I  E  N  N
N  H  O  E  E  R  T
S  O  W  L  I  O  S
```

All the answers are in the box; some are written from top to bottom, some from left to right, some from right to left and some diagonally.

b   Look again at the words you found in the puzzle in **a** and put the words into groups; you can group them in any way you like but your partner must try to guess why you have grouped them as you have.

—— 4 ——

a   In English you can build some compound nouns from two nouns like this:

You *open bottles* with a *bottle opener*.

Now think of some possible ways to finish the following compound nouns:

a tin
a knife
a coffee
a potato
a dish
a food

Check in your dictionary to see which of your words exist in English.

b   Of course, there are lots of gadgets and tools around the house for which we have a word which does not follow this pattern.

Example:
A *food cutter* is called a *knife* in English, **not** a *food cutter*.

What are the real words in English for the following invented words?

1 a clothes washer   ....
2 a nail hitter   ....
3 a cork remover   ....
4 a wood cutter   ....
5 clothes flattener   ....
6 a screw turner   ....
7 paper cutter   ....
8 a hole maker   ....
9 a picture taker   ....
10 a door locker   ....

SELF-STUDY ACTIVITIES

1 Find an object at home which you do not know the word for in English. Find the English word and think how you can explain it in English in your next lesson. Explain the word to the other members of the class.

2 You are thinking of decorating your bedroom. Make a list of the things you may need to buy.

3 For your next lesson find out the names of the following types of accommodation.

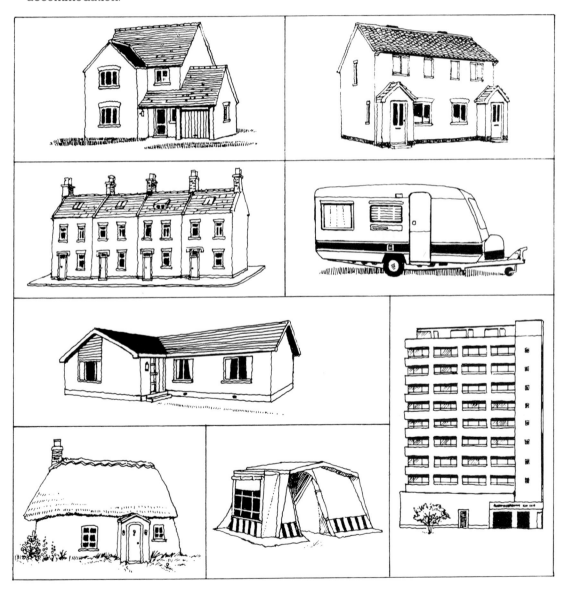

4 Finding partners for words: Collocation

We often combine words in certain ways. In English, for example, we can say:

heavy rain   a strong wind   make a mistake   do one's homework

Other languages may use different adjectives or verbs with these nouns. It is important, therefore, to learn the different partners that words can have. This unit looks at some common examples.

—— 1 —————————————————————————————————

a Which adjectives in box A can you combine with the nouns in box B?

A		B	
close	serious	sleeper	salary
hard	high	disappointment	worker
strong	light	friend	accent
big	heavy	illness	smoker

b Move round the class and find someone who . . .

. . . is a .... sleeper.

. . . is a .... smoker.

. . . is a .... worker.

. . . has (or will have) a .... salary.

. . . doesn't think they have a .... foreign accent when they speak English.

. . . has had a .... illness in their life.

. . . has recently had a .... disappointment.

. . . has a .... friend of a different nationality.

———— 2 ————

a   There are a number of phrases in English containing two words joined by *and*. The order of the words is usually fixed:

Examples:
here and there (*not* 'there and here')
fish and chips (*not* 'chips and fish')

Look at the underlined phrases in the following sentences. Are the words in the right order? (A dictionary should help you.)

1 I love the <u>quiet and peace</u> of the country.
2 I don't know if the plan will work; we'll have to <u>wait and see</u>.
3 Is it in colour or <u>white and black</u>?
4 I bought some <u>shares and stocks</u> the other day.
5 I can't stand the <u>hustle and bustle</u> of city life.
6 It doesn't matter what she wears, she always looks so <u>neat and tidy</u>.
7 It's not easy to start your own business, because there are so many government <u>regulations and rules</u>.
8 Ambulances have to get to an accident quickly; it's often a matter of <u>death and life</u>.
9 I don't know if we'll sell all these radios; it's a question of <u>supply and demand</u>.
10 I don't know how this machine works, but I'm sure we'll find out by a process of <u>error and trial</u>.

b   Complete the following phrases. The answers can all be found in the box on the right. (They are hidden vertically or horizontally.)

toast and ....
profit and ....
back and ....
thunder and ....
rich and ....
gin and ....
ladies and ....
up and ....
right and ....
pros and ....

L	I	G	H	T	N	I	N	G
O	P	E	F	O	R	T	H	E
S	W	A	T	N	I	L	I	N
S	R	E	B	I	D	O	Y	T
T	O	P	N	C	O	N	S	L
E	N	O	L	H	W	U	P	E
A	G	O	F	E	N	A	C	M
M	A	R	M	A	L	A	D	E
P	L	E	V	E	R	T	O	N

c   All the phrases in **a** and **b** above are formed by:

1 Synonyms or near synonyms, e.g. *rules and regulations*; or
2 Opposites or near opposites, e.g. *rich and poor*; or
3 Things which often go together, e.g. *toast and marmalade*.

Organise the phrases in a and b under these headings.

3
---

a Read the following:

'The <u>fire broke out</u> on the third floor and <u>swept through</u> the rest of the building. <u>Damage</u> is <u>estimated</u> at £1m.'

It would be common to find some, or all, of the underlined words in a newspaper or television account of a fire.
   Combine words from each of the columns below into sentences you think would appear. Then finish each sentence in a logical way.

A	B	C	D
Detectives	hijacked	a house	and wounded ....
Terrorists	broke into	the killer	found ....
Thieves	investigating	an army post	and demanded ....
Rebel forces	hunting	the murder	warned ....
Police	attacked	a plane	and stole ....

b Choose one of the stories and continue it for another three or four sentences.

c When you have finished, find a partner who has written the same story. Do your stories contain any of the same words or phrases? Together, make a list of more words that you think might appear in this type of story.

4
---

a Which of the pairs of adjectives on the left can you use with the nouns on the right?

hot or mild	hot or cold	sea	cheese
sweet or dry	sweet or sour	curry	bed
strong or weak	strong or mild	water	wine
rough or calm	rough or smooth	cigarettes	tea
hard or soft	hard or easy	exam	orange
		skin	surface

b Now practise these combinations by contradicting your partner like this:

Your partner: This cheese is strong.
You: Do you think so? I thought it was quite mild.

SELF-STUDY ACTIVITIES

1 You should try to keep a record in your notebook of these common combinations. One way is to organise them around themes. Try it for this unit. Choose five or six themes (e.g. *money* or *people*), and see if you can fit most of the combinations in this unit into these themes.

2 During the next two weeks try to find two or three texts on a subject which interests you. Compare the texts and look for combinations which appear in at least two of the texts.

Examples:
'The government is launching a new campaign against . . .'
'The animals hunt their prey in . . .'
'Since they set up the company two years ago . . .'

3 Look at the underlined verbs in the following sentences. Why do you think students might use the wrong verb in these sentences? (They are correct here!)
a) I'm sorry I'm late – I missed the bus.
b) I've wasted a lot of time this week.
c) Did you do your homework last night?
d) It's very easy to make this mistake.
e) Where do I get off the bus?

Make a list of other things we can *miss, waste, do, make* and *get off* in English.

5   Travelling can be fun??

───── **1** ─────────────────────────────

a   During a flight, three suitcases came undone and some of the contents got mixed up. Look at the list of contents below, and decide which objects belong together. What can you deduce about the owner of each suitcase? (There are different possibilities, but you must finish with nine objects for each suitcase.)

sleeping bag	paper clips
electric shaver	anorak
suntan lotion	tin opener
ceramic vase	Walkman
map of the Algarve	waistcoat
two T-shirts	calculator
high-heeled shoes	silk blouse
hotel receipt	file
travelling iron	nail file
knife, fork and spoon	tights
woollen hat	umbrella
three silk ties	bikini
Finnish phrasebook	diary
cream for mosquito bites	

b   Choose a place that you would like to go to for a holiday, and then write down nine things your suitcase might contain. Try to choose objects which say something about your age, personality and interests. You may choose objects from the list above if you wish.

―――― **2** ――――――――――――――――――――――――――――

a Study the underlined words and phrases in the following sentences. What function do they have, and what happens when you remove them from the sentences? Are the sentences still grammatically correct? Does the meaning change?

1 a) It was <u>even</u> bigger than I expected.
  b) He's <u>even</u> smaller than I thought.
2 a) She was <u>absolutely</u> marvellous.
  b) It was <u>absolutely</u> tiny.
3 a) It's <u>by far</u> the best film I've seen.
  b) It's <u>by far</u> her longest book.
4 a) He seemed strange at first, but <u>actually</u> he is very nice.
  b) It looks expensive, but <u>in actual fact</u> it was quite cheap.
5 a) She didn't say anything <u>at all</u>.
  b) She gave me nothing <u>at all</u>.
6 a) If I ask him to do something, he does <u>exactly</u> the opposite.
  b) They copied down all the answers, which is <u>exactly</u> what I didn't want.
7 a) We had to cancel the holiday <u>just</u> because he had a cold.
  b) We had to pay £5 <u>just</u> for a cup of coffee and a sandwich.

b Find suitable places to insert the above words and phrases in the following dialogue. You can use some of the words and phrases more than once.

A: Did you enjoy your holiday, then?
B: No, it was dreadful.
A: Why?
B: Well, at the first hotel we stayed in, they put us in a room overlooking the main street, which was what we didn't want because neither of us sleeps very well when it's noisy.
A: Well, what about the little island you went to? That must have been quiet and it's supposed to be very beautiful, isn't it?
B: That's what we thought before we went, but we didn't like it. The beaches were filthy, and there was nothing to do in the evening. Anyway, we were only there for a couple of days before we went back to the mainland and rented a small cottage.
A: Ah, was that any better?
B: If anything, it was worse. We only had running water half the time, and had to walk a couple of miles to get a loaf of bread and some milk.
A: Didn't you go there for the bird sanctuary, though?
B: Yes, we spent a couple of days bird watching, and that was the most interesting part of the holiday.
A: Perhaps you should stay at home next year.

c Making a minimum number of changes, rewrite the dialogue so that it gives a very positive impression of the holiday.

—— 3 ——

a 🔊 Listen to the sentences on the cassette and match them with these pictures.

b 🔊 Now listen again and write down each of the sentences.

c With a partner write two dialogues; each dialogue must contain one of the sentences from the cassette.

─── **4** ───

a Anthony and Clare decided to go on the weekend break advertised below. Unfortunately, it was not very successful, and some of Clare's comments on the holiday are written by it. What part of the advertisement do each of the comments refer to?

A SPECIAL WEEKEND BREAK TO

PARIS

ONLY £49

Paris – the most romantic city in the world. Treat yourself to a beautiful weekend away in a city made for lovers. See the Eiffel Tower, visit the Notre Dame Cathedral and take a river cruise on the Seine. Come to Paris with us – it's a marvellous weekend, exceptionally good value for money and an experience never to be forgotten.

COACH DEPARTS FRIDAYS 22nd AUGUST, 19th SEPTEMBER, 17th OCTOBER, 14th NOVEMBER, 12th DECEMBER.

Our special coach departs from Ealing on Friday evenings for the drive to Dover and the overnight sailing to Calais. We travel through the night on our comfortable coach, arriving at Paris at breakfast time. You are then free to discover Paris at leisure until mid-afternoon, or join our optional guided tour, taking in most of the major sights with stops for sightseeing. You'll have time to climb the Eiffel Tower, take a cruise on the river Seine and we include a visit to the Gragonard parfumerie. We check into our excellent 3 star hotel mid-afternoon for a rest. In the evening we take you to the Latin Quarter where you will have free time for dinner in one of the many fine restaurants. Return to the hotel late evening, taking in some more of the sights of Paris by night en route. Sunday morning after continental breakfast we check out of the hotel and visit the Place du Tertre and the Sacre Coeur. We leave Paris after lunch for the drive to Calais and the return ferry, arriving in Dover early evening and then return home.

1 We spent most of the time getting lost.

2 It was draughty, and the toilet was out of order.

3 Stale bread and coffee.

4 I was sick for most of the crossing.

5 We got a flat tyre on the way.

6 I was exhausted by the time we reached the top.

7 It was delicious but cost a fortune.

8 We argued most of the time.

9 The central heating wasn't working; we were frozen.

e.g. 8 →

b Everything Clare said was true, but Anthony thinks that Clare exaggerated the problems and forgot to mention the positive things. How do you think he would have expressed each of the above points?

Example:
1 We spent a bit of time getting lost, but we discovered some fascinating places.

C   Work in groups of three. One of you is Anthony, one is Clare, and the third person is a friend who is thinking of going on the same weekend break. Talk about the weekend.

SELF-STUDY ACTIVITIES

1 Based on your own experiences, make a list of six things that have gone wrong while you have been travelling, e.g. *I lost my luggage.*
   In the next lesson find out which is the most common travel problem in your class.

2 What is the difference between:

   a) *a coach* and *a bus?*
   b) *a hotel* and *a youth hostel?*
   c) *postponed* and *cancelled?*
   d) *run out of petrol* and *run short of petrol?*
   e) *break down* and *have a puncture?*
   f) *overbooked* and *overdue?*
   g) *full board* and *half board?*
   h) *a boarding card* and *a landing card?*

3 Imagine you are Anthony or Clare in Exercise **4**. Write a letter to a friend telling them about your weekend in Paris.

4 What is the missing preposition in the following sentences, and how many different meanings of this preposition can you find in the sentences? Can you use the same preposition for all of these meanings in your own language?

   a) We should be there .... four o'clock.

   b) We rented a cottage .... the lake.

   c) In the end we decided to go .... car.

   d) We can reserve the tickets .... phone.

   e) The cathedral was designed .... Gaudi.

   f) He makes a living .... selling souvenirs to tourists.

   g) .... the time we got there they had sold out.

   h) The tourist information office is .... the car park.

   i) The orchestra was conducted .... Bernstein.

   j) We got in .... climbing over the fence.

6 Revision and expansion

In this unit you are going to revise vocabulary from the first five units, but you will also be learning some new vocabulary as well.

——— 1 ———————————————————————————

When you go shopping, you often get a carrier bag for your shopping. Which of the items below do you think you could fit into two carrier bags? Work with a partner.

tin opener	tube of toothpaste	dishwasher	anorak
loaf of bread	pair of tights	file (for your school things)	
single blanket	small vase	stapler	silk shirt
bunch of flowers	pocket screwdriver	wrapping paper	hammer
box of paper clips	plug	coffee grinder	

——— 2 ———————————————————————————

Choose a suitable noun from the following list to complete each of the sentences below:

knife	vase	car	door	plants
sheet	carpet	things	toast	rubbish

1 Did you unlock the ....?

2 I think I've cracked the ....

3 I'm afraid I've burnt the ....

4 I think you'll have to sharpen the ....

5 Have you emptied the ....?

6 I think I've dented the front of the ....

7 I have to stay in and pack my ....

8 I hope the ink won't stain the ....

9 I'm afraid I've torn your best ....

10 I'm just going to water the ....

——— 3 ———

a [cassette] In some English words there are letters which are not pronounced, e.g. know and listen. Find the silent letters in the following words and then listen to the recording to check your answers.

wrap	receipt	calm	fasten	comb	hour	cupboard
comfortable	dictionary	knee				

b How many different words can you create using these silent letters? You can use the same letter more than once.

——— 4 ———

[cassette] Listen to the cassette and write down the words you hear. Find the words in the previous units (or use a dictionary) to check your spelling. Listen to the words again and practise the pronunciation.

——— 5 ———

a Think of any suitable statements or questions from A that would produce the following replies from B:

Example:

A: ....*Thank you*.... → B: Not at all.

1 A: .... B: Yes, you too.

2 A: .... B: No, I'm afraid I haven't.

3 A: .... B: Yes, help yourself.

4 A: .... B: Never mind, don't worry.

5 A: .... B: Yes, I'd love to.

6 A: .... B: Well, thanks anyway.

7 A: .... B: Oh, that's very kind of you.

8 A: .... B: You're kidding!

9 A: .... B: I don't mind.

10 A: .... B: Very well, thanks. And you?

b Practise the dialogues with a partner. Give your partner any of the questions or statements from A, and see if he or she can give you a suitable reply (without looking at the book).

6

The picture below is of a large hotel in the English countryside. Write a short text describing the wonderful facilities at the hotel. Imagine you are writing it for a travel brochure. Do not write more than 120 words, and try to use as many of the words and phrases in the box as you can.

peace and quiet	overlooking	a break	hustle and bustle
stressful	golf course	spend your time (-*ing*)	exactly
get away (from)	superb	first-class	efficient
elegant	views (of)	terrace	
balcony	beautifully furnished		

────── **7** ──────

One way of organising and recording new vocabulary is through pairs of
opposites or synonyms. Look at the words and phrases in the following box
and find *either* a synonym *or* an opposite for each one. When you have
finished, compare your answers with a partner and discuss the differences.

blunt	there's plenty to do	a light sleeper	profit	dirty
first language	lazy	to fill	to pass	wealthy
tactful	neat	to defend	rules	efficient

────── **8** ──────

Complete the columns below:

Noun suffixes   *Adjective suffixes*

-tion   e.g. education   -ive   e.g. attractive

....   e.g. ....   e.g. ....

....   e.g. ....   e.g. ....

....   e.g. ....   e.g. ....

Compare your answers with your partner and write down three more examples
for each suffix.

────── **9** ──────

What is the opposite of the following?

1 a high salary ....

2 a sweet orange ....

3 a slight accent ....

4 a minor illness ....

5 fresh bread ....

6 a slight disappointment ....

7 strong coffee ....

8 a serious problem ....

9 strong cheese ....

10 a hot curry ....

11 a sweet wine ....

12 a slight cold ....

—— 10 ——

In this exercise you must change one four-letter word into a completely
different four-letter word in four moves. With each move you have to change
one letter from the previous word but still produce a real English word.

Example:

hall	fall	fill	file	fine

1	tent	....	....	....	ball
2	sick	....	....	....	part
3	fear	....	....	....	boot
4	foot	....	....	....	wind

—— 11 ——

How many examples of the following can you think of?

1 VEHICLES: car, bus ....

2 WEAPONS: ....

3 INSECTS: ....

4 TOOLS: ....

5 FURNITURE: ....

—— 12 ——

Write down three things you can . . .

1 win: money, a game, a competition ....

2 run: ....

3 miss: ....

4 catch: ....

5 run out of: ....

6 lose: ....

7 make: ....

8 do: ....

—— 13 ——

Look back at some of the ways of organising vocabulary in Unit 1
Exercise **1.** Can you produce your own examples of the seven ways of
grouping?

7 Money and finance

a Here is a story about some problems a man had with his bank. The sentences have been mixed up. Put them in the correct order, and add any other words you need to link the story together, e.g. *so, because,* etc.

He was overdrawn.	....
He opened a deposit account.	....
He got a statement in the post.	....
He forgot about his standing order for £50.	....
He paid for a new shirt by cheque.	....
He transferred £160 back to his current account.	....
He closed his deposit account.	....
He had £200 in his current account.	....**1**....
He had to pay bank charges.	....
He wanted to earn more interest on his savings.	....
He transferred £160 to his deposit account.	....

b The man paid for his new shirt by cheque. There are, of course, lots of ways of paying for things. Look at the following methods of payment. When do you use them?

1 Pay cash.
2 Pay by credit card.
3 Pay by cheque.
4 Pay by standing order.

Do you know any other ways of paying?

c Describe a cheque to someone who has never seen one before. What's on it? What do you write on it? What can you do with it? What can't you do with it?

—— 2 ——

You have £500. If you think one of the following sentences is correct, you can bet up to £50 that it is correct. If you think a sentence is wrong, you can bet up to £50 that it is wrong. You do not have to bet £50 each time. If you are right, you double your money. That means that you could finish with a maximum of £1,000. The winner is the person with the most money at the end. Now study the sentences and place your bets.*

 1 I have much money.
 2 I'm afraid I've forgotten my wallet at home.
 3 I've run out of money.
 4 Could you borrow me £50?
 5 I really need £50, but I could make do with £30.
 6 I'm study economic at university.
 7 It's not worth to spend a lot of money.
 8 I've got a brand new car.
 9 I bought it last week because my other one was completely damaged.
10 If you've got the money, you might as well spend it.
11 I've saved £100 since the last three months.
12 I'm afraid I haven't money enough to buy that coat.
13 I feel like a drink. Could you lend me 50 pence?
14 I'm afraid but it's too expensive.
15 I didn't learn anything on the course; I think I lost my time and my money.

*Exercise **2** is adapted from an idea in *Grammar Games* by Mario Rinvolucri, Cambridge University Press, 1984.

'Will you be paying by cheque, credit card, money, or are you shoplifting?'

—— **3** ——————————————————————

a   Look at the following graph and then read the five texts. Match the names of the five companies with the profit figures for that company. (These companies all produce photocopiers.)

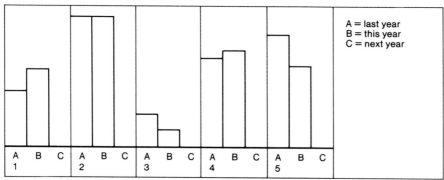

A = last year
B = this year
C = next year

Profit

It has been a good year for **MEM**. Sales fell slightly in the first quarter but then rose steadily throughout the rest of the year. This progress is not fully shown in the profit figures because the company made large investments in new machinery. However, the overall position still shows a small increase in profit for the year.

KWIK made a very successful entry into the market last year, but it has been unable to maintain that progress. Sales remained stable for the first six months but since then they have fallen sharply. Overall profit is down by 50%.

It has been a disappointing year for **Thomas Sayer**. With the introduction of the XR 3000 model, the company expected sales to rise sharply; unfortunately, the response to the new model has not been favourable. However, sales of the older models have risen slowly, so Sayer have been able to maintain the same profits as last year.

The 'Mini' copier introduced by **Renon** last year has been the fastest selling machine this year. Although it does not have the capacity of the larger photocopiers, it is very compact and extremely reliable. Sales were slow at first, but then rose sharply in the second half of the year. Profits are up on last year and the future looks healthy.

P & E have had a difficult period since the management reorganisation two years ago. Production problems delayed the introduction of their new model, and sales of the older models have fallen – slowly at first, and then quite sharply by the final quarter. However, the company are hoping for a much better profit position by the end of next year.

b   With the information above, indicate the approximate pattern for sales over the four quarters of this year.

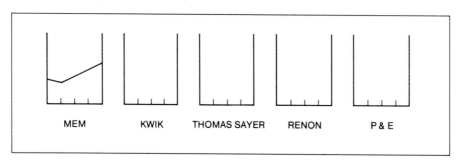

MEM   KWIK   THOMAS SAYER   RENON   P & E

c Now you are going to make a forecast. With the information you have, mark on the first graph the profit you forecast for each company next year. Compare your answers with a partner and discuss the differences.

d Can you think of any products in your country which . . .

1 . . . have fallen slightly in price over the last year?
2 . . . have fallen quite sharply in price over the last year?
3 . . . have risen sharply in price over the past year?
4 . . . have stayed the same price over the past year?
5 . . . you think will rise quite sharply in price over the next year?
6 . . . you think will stay the same price over the next year?

—— **4** ——————————————————————

a All the following statements are surprising; for example, a 5p piece isn't usually *worth a fortune*. With your partner, suggest explanations or situations in which you might hear each of the statements:

1 'So my 5p piece was worth a fortune!'
2 'That £2m was almost worthless, you see.'
3 'It only cost 25p but I insisted on a receipt.'
4 'There was nothing wrong with the wallet, but they had to give me a refund.'
5 'So, you see, I only paid £200 for the matchbox – a real bargain!'
6 'Well, I refused to pay cash; I wrote him a cheque for 2p!'
7 'I had never met her before but I was happy to give her the painting, even though it was quite valuable.'
8 'So, you see, even though it was a sale, I paid more than the normal price.'

b Working with your partner, think of a story using at least half of the following words:

a . . . piece	a bargain	worthless	a receipt	a wallet
a purse	a sale	a refund	pay cash	a cheque
valuable	the normal price		worth	

When you have finished, tell your story to another pair and make sure they have used the words correctly in their story.

SELF-STUDY ACTIVITIES

1. Organise the following words into different groups. You must decide what the groups are, and how many groups there are. In the next lesson, you must explain the reasons for your way of organising the words.

discount	fee	salary	bill	fare	bonus
price	income tax	refund	rent	pay rise	

2 In the following sentences, the verbs are used with 'money' expressions. If you change the 'money' expression to a 'time' expression, are the sentences still correct?

Example:
I spent £200 in Vienna.   →   I spent two weeks in Vienna.

a) I wasted a lot of money on that course.
b) We invested a lot of money in that project.
c) I inherited £5,000.
d) If we get a computer, we'll save a lot of money in the long term.
e) I found a £10 note in the street.

3 Complete the following sentences with *up* or *down*. Are there any sentences where both words are possible?

a) If profits are .... again this year, there could be redundancies.

b) If we put .... our prices, we'll be less competitive.

c) The rent has gone .... three times since we moved in.

d) Business was slow at first but things are picking .... now.

e) The government is hoping to keep inflation .... to 5% this year.

f) The economy was growing very fast at the beginning of the year but it's slowing .... a bit now.

8   Connecting words and ideas 1

——— 1 ———————————————————————————

a Organise the sentences below into a logical story:

She soon started talking.   ....

The salesman had resigned.   ....

I didn't ask her what the matter was.   ....

I was quite relieved to hear this news.   ....

Denise didn't say anything when she arrived.   ....

She'd had an argument with one of the sales staff. ....

She'd had a bad day at work.   ....

b We can make the story more complete, and more natural, by connecting
the ideas together with adverbs which also tell us something about the
speaker's/writer's attitude to the events. Choose a suitable adverb from the
box below to begin each of the sentences:

unfortunately	apparently	to be honest	obviously
fortunately	naturally	to my surprise	

——— 2 ———————————————————————————

a We often repeat information in a text but choose different words to do
so. Can you find synonyms in the following article for the words which are
underlined in the text?

Holiday travellers faced long delays today after a French air traffic control dispute and a double computer failure threw Europe's airways into chaos.

A number of flights were held up for more than six hours and one group of holidaymakers was unable to leave Portugal today, as scheduled. So far, they have been stranded at Faro Airport for more than 20 hours.

A row over working conditions is responsible for the problems with the French air traffic control, but the confusion has been made worse by the simultaneous breakdown of important computers at Brest and Prestwick.

b In the following story, find the best synonym from the list to replace the words which are underlined in the text:

well-off	meat	a bit of a shock	money	as	trouble
butcher's	told me	embarrassed	revolting	met	
frightened	apparently	children	friends	animal	

I bumped into an old colleague of mine yesterday. His name is Oliver Knight, but he was always known as 'OK' to his <u>colleagues</u>. I <u>bumped into</u> him buying liver in a shop down the road. Now this was surprising because OK is a strict vegetarian and has always felt that <u>liver</u> is disgusting. 'It's for the kids,' he said by way of explanation.

This too was <u>surprising because</u> OK had always been a bachelor and certainly hadn't had time to become a father since I last saw him. 'They're my wife's from a previous marriage,' he <u>said</u> shyly.

It turned out that he had married someone called Petra, and she had come complete with a family – a boy and a girl, and a dog. I knew that OK was scared of dogs, so I asked him how he managed. <u>It turned out that</u> he had been <u>scared</u> at first, but now they were the best of friends; in fact, the huge <u>dog</u> I had seen waiting outside the <u>shop</u> was the <u>dog</u> in question.

'It must have affected your finances, taking on a family,' I said. You see, OK wasn't a wealthy man.

He looked a little <u>shy</u> for a moment. '<u>Finance</u> isn't a problem. Petra's rather <u>wealthy</u>, you see, and she's got a very good job,' he said. 'The <u>problem</u> is that I stay at home and have to cook all this <u>disgusting</u> meat for the <u>kids</u>.'

c Two words may act as synonyms in one text, but that does not mean they are exactly the same. There are many possible differences:

1 One word is more general than the other, e.g. *seat* is more general than *armchair*.
2 One word is more formal or colloquial than the other, e.g. *guy* is more colloquial than *man*.
3 One word is more common than the other, e.g. *terrible* is more common than *ghastly*.
4 The meaning may be similar in one context but not in another, e.g. you can say *a busy shop* and *a crowded shop*. You can say *a busy day at work* but **not** *a crowded day at work*.
5 The words have the same meaning, but different grammar, e.g. *Can I borrow your pen?*, but *Can you lend me your pen?*

Look back at the synonyms in **a** and **b**. How many examples of 1–5 above can you find?

——— 3 ———————————————————

a Look at the two headlines and then choose the words and phrases from the box which you would expect to see in each story. Are there any words which would probably appear in both stories? Use a dictionary to help you.

DRIVER CRASHES INTO PLANE

12 killed in motorway fire

inferno	jet	a pile-up	a bruise/to bruise
to tow	to swerve	to burst into flames	wing
to dazzle	horrific	inquiry	concussed/concussion
tractor	a write-off	wreckage	severe burns
victims	unharmed	a leak/to leak	petrol

b Compare your answers with a partner and explain why you have grouped the words in this particular way.

c   Now read the two texts and see how the words are used.

DRIVER CRASHES INTO PLANE

BRUISED motorist Julie Fuller was nursing her dented pride yesterday after smashing into a £5 million pound PLANE.

Julie's fireman husband Roy raced to the crash scene to find her injured in the wreckage.

Their car was a write-off and the jet's wing was damaged. But the couple's baby son Bryn luckily escaped unharmed.

And last night, as air chiefs began an inquiry, concussed Julie was making a good recovery in hospital.

Julie, 27, had been driving along the perimeter road of Surrey's Dunsfold airfield.

She was about to pick up Roy when she was dazzled by the lights of an on-coming tractor towing a Hawk trainer jet.

Julie swerved round the tractor, but slammed into the plane's wing.

Roy, 31, said: "I was first on the scene and it was a terrible shock.

"The car was badly damaged and she had head injuries.

"When I spoke to her later in hospital, she could only remember the dazzling lights."

A British Aerospace spokesman said: "An inquiry has been launched.

"We are just very grateful that Mrs Fuller was not more seriously injured."

12 killed in motorway fire

TWELVE people died and six were injured in a horrific motorway inferno yesterday.

Petrol leaking from eight wrecked vehicles burst into flames in the M61 pile-up, engulfing cars and trucks.

Four children were among the dead, and police said that identifying the victims would be difficult because of their severe burns.

The accident happened at a notorious blackspot under a bridge at a new junction near Bamber Bridge, south of Preston, Lancs.

Hours later the motorway was still closed because of fears that the fire-damaged bridge would collapse and emergency services worked under floodlights to clear the gutted debris from the road.

d   With a partner, prepare a short newspaper story to go with one of the headlines below. When you have finished, give ten key words from your story to another pair and see if they can construct your story. You can use words and phrases from the above texts.

Three dead in hotel bomb blast

POLICE CAR CHASE ENDS IN TRAGEDY

Miraculous escape as plane crashes on motorway

SELF-STUDY ACTIVITIES

1 Find two texts in an English textbook or newspaper, and see if you can find
  four to six examples of synonymy in each text, i.e. examples of different
  words and phrases being used in the text to express the same idea.

2 Write a newspaper article to accompany one of the headlines in Exercise **3d**.

3 Find synonyms in this unit for the words in the box below. Say whether the
  synonym is more formal or colloquial or whether it is more or less general in
  meaning:

employee	of course	to injure	explosion	aeroplane
vehicle	fire	actually	to pull	OK
caused	travellers	an argument	to inform	

9 Communicating with people

— 1 —

a Here are some communication problems. Match the sentences on the left with a suitable reply from the right:

1 I can't hear what she's saying.
2 I didn't understand that explanation at all.
3 I can't get through.
4 What did she say her name was?
5 She speaks incredibly fast.
6 I think she misunderstood what I said.

a) Why? Is it engaged?
b) Well, tell her again.
c) Well, ask her to speak up a bit.
d) I'm afraid I didn't catch it either.
e) Well, ask her to slow down a bit.
f) Well, ask her to go over it again.

b Practise these short dialogues with a partner.

'Yes. Will you accept a collect call from a Mr Aaaaaaaaaa?'

— 2 —

a We often use the word *thing(s)* when we cannot or do not want to be precise, and especially when the speaker and listener know what *thing* refers to. What do you think *thing(s)* might refer to in the following sentences?

1 Could you turn that thing down a bit? It's giving me a headache.
2 You should put those things away after you've ironed them.
3 It was so painful I couldn't swallow a thing.
4 When you're a public figure, a thing like this can be very damaging.
5 I used to like Peter very much but things are different now.
6 You'd better put those things in the fridge or they'll go off.

38

b Read the following dialogue and use the clues to work out what the *thing* is:

A: Where did you get that thing?
B: I found it on the bus; it must have fallen out of someone's pocket.
A: It's a rather nasty thing to be carrying around with you, don't you think?
B: Yes, and this blade is really sharp.

c With a partner, prepare a four-line dialogue about one of the things in the following box. Provide clues to the meaning but don't actually use the word. When you have finished, read your dialogue to another pair. Can they guess your word?

a microwave	a house plant	a vase of flowers	a calculator
a ruler	a food mixer	your wallet (you've lost it)	
your purse (you've lost it)		a diary	a calendar

—— **3** ——

a Some English words for types of communication are easily confused. Look at the following words with their dictionary definitions. Do you understand the differences in meaning, and can you find any pairs of words which you think are almost identical in meaning?

argument /ˈɑːgjəˈmənt/, **arguments**. 1 An argument is a set of statements in support of an opinion or proposed course of action. It is expressed in an orderly way, and is used to try to convince someone that the opinion or course of action is correct. EG *Do you accept this argument?... There are strong arguments against these measures... Perhaps more common is the argument that disarmament agreements cannot work.*
2 An **argument** is also a disagreement over a particular matter between two or more people, sometimes resulting in them shouting angrily at each another. EG *He and David had been drawn into a ferocious argument about their jointly owned car... I said no and we got into a big argument over it.*

chat /tʃæt/
2 A **chat** is an informal, friendly conversation, usually about things which are not serious or important. EG *We had a nice long chat about our schooldays... My friends often come in for coffee and a chat.*

conversation /kɒnvəˈseɪʃən/, **conversations**. 1 If you have a **conversation** with someone, you talk with them in an informal situation. EG *Roger and I had a conversation about fishing... I had a long telephone conversation with my father... He spent some hours in conversation with me... She made no attempt to get into conversation with her neighbour.*

discussion /dɪskʌʃən/
2 A **discussion** is a conversation, speech, or piece of writing in which a subject is considered in detail, from several points of view. EG *John Lyons will be taking part in a discussion on 'Language and Communication'... We have had discussions with Members of Parliament about the new immigration laws.*

lecture /lɛktʃə/, **lectures, lecturing, lectured**. 1 A **lecture** is a talk on a particular subject that is given in order to teach people about that subject, for example by a university or college teacher. EG *...a series of lectures on literature... I went to a lecture he gave at the African Institute... ...lecture notes.*

lesson /lɛsən/, **lessons**. 1 A **lesson** is 1.1 a short period of time when people are taught about a particular subject or taught how to do a particular activity. EG *...tennis lessons... ...a history lesson.*

⟫⟶

39

row /raʊ/
6 A **row** is 6.1 a noisy argument, especially between people in the same family or people who know each other very well; an informal use. EG *They were always having terrible rows... ...a family row.* 6.2 a serious disagreement or dispute about a public matter such as a government policy, especially when it is described in newspapers and on television and radio; an informal use. EG *This was basically a political row... A new row has broken out over the government's plans to cut spending on the health service.*

speech /spiːtʃ/
2 A **speech** is 2.1 a formal talk which someone gives to an audience, and which they have usually prepared in advance. EG *Mr Macmillan presented the prizes and made a speech on the importance of education... He gave a very amusing speech at her wedding... We listened to an excellent speech by the president.*

Collins COBUILD English
Language Dictionary

b Study the following sentences. Decide what type of communication they are (using the words above), and then finish each sentence in a logical way:

1 '. . . we're going to miss Daniel very much, but I'm sure you'll all join me in wishing him the very best of luck in ....'

2 '. . . why did you tell Mum that I was planning to go to the party on Saturday? You knew she'd be furious if she found out. Honestly, Sarah, I could ....'

3 '. . . you're absolutely right about the dangers of drug addiction, but I think you need to make a distinction between hard drugs ....'

4 '. . . well, we're thinking of buying a new fridge-freezer, but apart from that ....'

5 '. . . I'd just like to outline the major problems first, and then I'll go back and look at some of these problems in ....'

c Which of the following verbs and adjectives could you use with the nouns in **a**?

	Verbs	
have	make	give

Adjectives		
brief	long	formal
terrible	fantastic	heated
amusing	boring	furious

Example:
You <u>have</u> a conversation, and the conversation could be <u>brief</u>, <u>long</u>, <u>amusing</u>, <u>boring</u> or even <u>terrible</u>.

—— **4** ——

a Two ways of communicating are by letter and by cassette letter. Which of the following statements are true of a letter, and which are true of a cassette letter? Discuss this in groups.

1 It's cheaper.   4 It's more satisfying.
2 It's easier.   5 It's more enjoyable for the person who receives it.
3 It's more personal.

b John has been working in Brazil for six weeks. Read the letter that he sent to his sister, Julie, and then answer the questions below.

Hotel Laranjeiras
Rio de Janeiro

24 March

Dear Julie,

I'm sorry I haven't written for a while, but I've been incredibly busy at work and have spent virtually all my spare time looking for a flat. Anyway, the good news is that I may have found somewhere at last. I saw a really nice place this morning – a third floor flat with two bedrooms and a huge lounge. To be honest, I can't really afford it, but there's an American guy I know who is also looking for accommodation so I'll see if he'd like to share. If not, I'll probably take up Eduardo's offer because I'm getting pretty fed up with living in this hotel.

My other good news is that I met a very nice Brazilian couple the other night and they've invited me to spend a weekend with them at their house in the country. It'll be nice to get away from Rio for a couple of days. The only problem is that they don't speak much English, and my Portuguese is still pretty basic – anyway, I'll let you know how I get on.

By the time you read this letter you'll have got my cassette letter and heard about my embarrassing experience last week. Well, I saw João yesterday – he told me that Brazilians have very big appetites and he apologised for trying to make me eat so much. I felt so stupid I didn't have the courage to tell him the truth.

By the way, I can't remember if I thanked you for the things you sent me. Believe me, they'll be really handy when I get a flat and start doing a bit of cooking for myself.

I'm afraid I'll have to finish now. Sorry it's a short letter but I've arranged to go out with some friends. I'll write again at the end of the week. Until then, take care of yourself and give my love to Garfield.

Love, John

---

1 What do you think Eduardo's offer might be?
2 What do you think the embarrassing experience might have been?
3 What 'things' do you think Julie sent him?
4 Who do you think Garfield might be?
5 Can you think of words or phrases that could be used to replace the following words and phrases from the letter?

virtually	spare (time)	huge	I can't really afford it
fed up (with)	I'll let you know how I get on		

⟫→

c 🖭 Now listen to the cassette letter that John sent to Julie. Write down the correct answers to questions 1–4 above and one other fact that you learn about Julie.

d Look at the way the following words and phrases are used in both the letter and the cassette letter. Do they have the same meaning each time they are used, and can you find a single translation for each one?

pretty   anyway   by the way   handy

SELF-STUDY ACTIVITIES

1 What sort of messages are you communicating when you do the following?

scream	clap	cry	smile
whisper	nod	whistle	cheer

Example:
cry: You are probably very unhappy or possible extremely happy.

2 Imagine you are John (from Exercise **4**). Write the next letter (or make the next cassette letter) that John sent to his sister. Think about the following:

a) What happened about the flat?
b) What happened during the weekend visit to the country?
c) Have you spoken to Joao again?

Include at least one new piece of information. In your next lesson, exchange letters or cassette letters with a partner and compare them.

3 Think of a text you have read this week (either in English or in your first language) and then try to summarise it in English. You can do this in your head (without writing it down) when you have a few spare minutes (e.g. on the way to class). If you find it difficult to remember any of the vocabulary, check it later with the text or with a dictionary.

10 One + one = three: Compounds

a Look at these examples:

One word + *One word* = *New word*

alarm + clock = alarm clock (a compound noun)
easy + going = easy-going (a compound adjective)
baby + sit = to babysit (a compound verb)

The most common type of compound is a compound noun, and you can often create compound nouns in English by using your first language and a little imagination. For example, how many compound nouns can you find using the following words? (Use a dictionary to check your answers.)

Example:
...*credit*... card .... paper .... room .... chair

a Look at the compound nouns in the box below. Would you find them . . .

. . . under the bonnet?
. . . in the boot?
. . . inside the car?
. . . outside the car?

a number plate	a seat belt	a tool kit	a handbrake
an ashtray	a car key	a clutch pedal	a steering wheel
driving gloves	a passenger seat	a spare wheel	windscreen wipers
a petrol engine	a door handle	a petrol tank	

b Now look at the second part of each compound (i.e. *plate, belt, kit*, etc.) and try to think of more examples of compound nouns using these words.

───── **3** ─────────────────────────────

a Match words in the left-hand box with words in the right-hand box to form 16 compound nouns describing different hobbies and leisure activities.

hang	stamp	sun
water	rifle	motor
weight	window	
oil	dress	
sight	bird	
parachute	baby	
rock	wind	

watching	shooting	sitting
painting	cycling	gliding
making	climbing	seeing
collecting	surfing	jumping
skiing	shopping	
training	bathing	

b Move round the class and find out if anyone does any of these things. If so, find out more about this particular hobby or activity.

───── **4** ─────────────────────────────

a Can you find a word to go in each of the brackets below, so that you have a compound with the word before the brackets and a compound with the word after the brackets?

Example:

top (....*speed*....) limit

lunch (....................) table

shop (....................) manager

toilet (....................) towel

phone   (.........................) plate

wheel   (.........................) person

burglar   (.........................) clock

window   (.........................) list

bed   (.........................) service

table   (.........................) racket

soft   (.........................) house

identity (.........................) board

b Now write sentences which combine both of the compounds in each case.

Example:
You can't go at top speed in most cars in Britain because the speed limit is only 70 m.p.h.

SELF-STUDY ACTIVITIES

1 Write the first half of five compound words (from this unit) on a piece of paper. On another piece of paper write the *second* half of five *different* compound words. Each day for a week look at your two pieces of paper and see if you can remember the other half of the compounds in each case.

2 Building compounds from common words (as you did in Exercise **1**) is a quick and easy way to expand your vocabulary. Try it for these words and then check your answers in a dictionary.

sun.........................   ....time   ....book

11 Man and nature

— 1 —

a You are going to read a text about the problems that zoos face in caring for rare animals. Before you read it, look at the words in the box below. Do you think these words are *certain* to be in the text, *likely* to be in the text, or *unlikely* to be in the text?

disappearance	in danger of extinction	otherwise	witness	endanger
rare	in captivity	protect	breed	restricted
explode	goal	mammals		

Now read the text and see if you were right.

The captive costs

According to Dr William Conway, director of the New York Zoo and chairman of the American Association of Zoological Parks and Aquariums, modern zoos can do a great deal to serve as a backup strategy to support the primary conservation goal of safeguarding species in their wild habitats. No less and no more.

Zoos are severely limited in terms of sheer space, let alone animal care capacity. All the animal space in the world's zoos would comfortably fit inside the Inner London Circular. They now contain rather more than half a million individual mammals, birds, reptiles and amphibians. During the past few years they have bred about 9 per cent of all 8,700 bird species, and 19 per cent of all 4,500 mammal species.

Not all of these are yet threatened or rare creatures: this is the case for only 12 per cent of the birds and 48 per cent of the mammals. But the number of endangered forms is expanding rapidly.

It is an expensive business to

care for threatened animals. To look after one Siberian tiger costs almost £2,000 a year, which means that to care for an expected total of 500 Siberian tigers in the world's zoos over a period of 20 years will cost almost £20 million.

Gorillas are even more costly: the 500 in zoos cost £2,850 each per year, making a total of £28 million over 20

years. Unless we can keep them alive in captivity, we shall probably witness, within the coming decades, the demise of around 100 large carnivore species, some 160 species of primates, and perhaps 215 herbivores other than primates, plus about 300 species from other mammalian orders, making a total of about 800 species.

b   Look back at the words which did not appear in the text. How many of these words can you put into the text by making small changes in the text? (The meaning must stay the same.)

c   In groups discuss the following statement:

'I think it's terrible to spend all this money on tigers and gorillas when there are millions of people starving in the world. And in any case, it's very cruel to keep lions and tigers and other big animals in a restricted space in a zoo.'

——— 2 ———————————————————

a   Find out the names of the animals below:

b   Which of the adjectives in the box below do you normally associate with each of the species in **a**? Are there any words you cannot use to describe an animal? If so, why not? Work with a partner and use a dictionary if necessary.

ugly	aggressive	powerful	elegant	nervous	cunning
clumsy	proud	agile	shy	easy-going	
selfish	stubborn	independent	unpleasant	emotional	

c   Imagine the species in **a** were all endangered animals. Which ones would you most like to preserve, and why? Discuss in groups.

—— **3** ————————————————————————————

a 🔲 You are going to listen to an interview about the problems facing the panda population in China. These problems are summarised in the following notes but some of the information is wrong. Read the notes first and then listen to the interview. Note down the mistakes.

1 Hunters set traps for the pandas and kill them.
2 Farmers destroy the forests which provide the pandas with food.
3 Leopards, foxes and wild dogs sometimes kill young pandas.
4 Some pandas die in floods.
5 A disease called *Ascaris Shroederi* doesn't harm male pandas but can kill females.
6 Pandas travel a long way in search of food but they still die from starvation because they have enormous appetites and require enormous quantities of food to survive.
7 Pandas breed regularly but the parents often reject the young cubs and they are then killed by other animals.

b 🔲 Listen to the second part of the interview. When it has finished, look at the following tapescript of the interview. There are ten mistakes. Can you find them?

. . . So after mating the mail may disappear for ever, leaving the female to do all the work. When she is ready to give birth – sometime in the autumn – she will find, or create, a whole in the trunk of an old tree and build a kind of nest. This accounts for the number of hollowed out trees that can be scene in these forests. A normal litter may be a single cub, sometimes too, and very occasionally three – but sadly only won will survive because the maternal care needed is sew great that only a single cub can be looked after. The rejected cubs will certainly dye from the cold, starvation, or possibly other predators.

But that's not all. When the cub is born it ways just 100 grams and is only ten centimetres long; that's between 900 and 1,000 times smaller than its mother. The wait doubles within a weak but it's still tiny. This is another very important . . .

—— ┤ **SELF-STUDY ACTIVITIES** ├ ————————————————————

1 The verbs in the lists below have all appeared in this unit. Using a dictionary, find the nouns formed from these verbs:

Verb	Noun		Verb	Noun
solve	*solution*		survive	
starve			rescue	
protect			restrict	
explode			trap	
preserve			reduce	

2 Find a newspaper story in your first language. Without reading it, make a list
  of about ten words which you expect to find in the story (like the list in
  Exercise **1a**). Now read it and use a dictionary to find the English equivalents
  of the words which are in the text.

3 Find out the following facts about your country:

  a) Are there any protected animals in your country?
  b) Are there any animals which are killed as pests in your country?
  c) Do you need a licence to keep any animals in your country?
  d) Are there any kinds of meat which are not eaten in your country?
  e) Which animals are kept on farms in your country?

  In your next lesson discuss these questions in groups and find out if there are
  any animals – big or small – that people in your class are frightened of.

12   Revision and expansion

In this unit you are going to revise vocabulary from Units 7 to 11, but you will also be learning some new vocabulary.

—— 1 ——————————————————————

Add one word to the following groups to form three compound words in each case:

1 identity / credit / birthday ....*card*............

2 phrase / exercise / address ....

3 toilet / news / writing ....

4 cloak / waiting / spare ....

5 bank / cheque / deposit ....

6 rocking / arm / wheel ....

7 spare / part / lunch ....

8 bedside / dressing / coffee ....

Now add one more example to each group.

—— 2 ——————————————————————

a Find the 15 pairs of approximate synonyms in the box below:

obviously	rescue	hungry	handy	worker
lend	nasty	say	cost a fortune	tell
unpleasant	save	rare	valuable	useful
radiator	employee	borrow	furious	expensive
starving	meat	unusual	central heating	liver
be held up	worth a fortune	naturally	angry	delay

b With a partner, discuss how these synonyms are slightly different in meaning.

Example:

Employee is a more formal word than *worker*.

—— 3 ——

a  Listen carefully to the pronunciation of the endings of the following words and then practise saying them with a partner:

ow<u>ner</u>   act<u>or</u>   dark<u>ness</u>   happi<u>ness</u>
nerv<u>ous</u>   deli<u>cious</u>   dam<u>age</u>   lugg<u>age</u>
secret<u>ary</u>   hist<u>ory</u>   reli<u>able</u>   predict<u>able</u>

b Now think of two more words for each of the six different endings and practise the pronunciation.

—— 4 ——

a Explain the context or situation in which you might hear the following:

Example:

Did you realise there was a 30 m.p.h. speed limit, sir?	*Context:* It could be a policeman or policewoman speaking, having just stopped a motorist for driving too fast.

 1 I'm afraid you're overdrawn, Mrs Clark.
 2 Look, it's leaking all over the kitchen floor.
 3 Do you have the receipt, madam?
 4 Look, if we don't find a garage, we could be stranded here for hours.
 5 Sorry, could you speak up a bit – it's a bad line?
 6 Well, it hurts when I swallow.
 7 I'll just check the steering, and then you can pick it up after lunch.
 8 To be honest, I think it was a choice of either resign or be sacked.
 9 I'm afraid I couldn't get through – it's engaged.
10 I just heard a loud crash and then it burst into flames.

b With a partner, build conversations around one or two of these situations.

'So it's powerful.
I still don't want one'

⬛ 5

Listen to the cassette and write down the words you hear. Find the words in the previous units (or use a dictionary) to check your spelling. Listen to the words again and practise your pronunciation.

6

Look at the following pairs of adjectives. Are they often used together to describe a person and/or an animal? Work with a partner and use the scale below to indicate your answers.

Scale: very common
           quite common
           perhaps
           unlikely
           highly unlikely

1 shy and nervous
2 cunning and selfish
3 nervous and aggressive
4 stubborn and easy-going

5 proud and stubborn
6 tactless and insensitive
7 agile and clumsy
8 aggressive and tactless

7

Complete the following sentences with the correct prepositions:

1 It won't finish until ten o'clock .... the earliest.

2 I haven't seen her .... a while.

3 It'll be dark .... the time we get home.

4 I looked .... their pets while they were .... holiday.

5 I spent a lot of money .... petrol last week.

6 I'm afraid we've run out .... coffee.

7 We're thinking .... going to Greece next year.

8 He was turning right .... the traffic lights .... Camborne Road, and he crashed .... a Mercedes which was coming .... the opposite direction.

8

Complete and extend the following network:

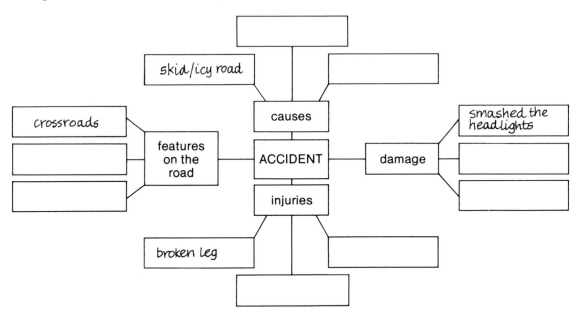

9

With a partner discuss the sequence of actions in starting a car, and then compare your answer with another pair. The first two steps are given below:

1 Unlock the door.
2 Get in.

10

Look at the problems in each column below. Which do you worry about most and why?

Personal problems	*World problems*
Traffic congestion in your village, town or city	The debt problems of developing countries
The danger of being in a road accident	Pollution
Your own money worries	Preservation of endangered species
Your future (at school, university or work)	Natural disasters such as earthquakes or famine
Learning English	
Your health	

————— **11** ——————————————————————————

a In Unit 11 you looked at different words with the same pronunciation, e.g. *mail/male*. Find words with the same pronunciation as the following:

week / ...*weak*...   blue / ....   sail / ....
stair / ....   steal / ....   toe / ....
wait / ....   fair / ....   flew / ....
so / ....   which / ....   pair / ....
die / ....   break / ....   threw / ....

b Write a short story including at least six of the above words. Then read your story slowly to two partners while they write it down. At the end, compare the three written accounts.

————— **12** ——————————————————————————

a Here is a quiz to test your memory of the last five units. Write down your answers:

1 In Unit 7 a man had a problem with his bank. What was the problem?
2 In Unit 8 you read a text about a driver who crashed into a jet plane. How did it happen?
3 In Unit 8 you also read a story about Oliver Knight. What can you remember about his life?
4 In Unit 9 you listened to John's cassette letter to his sister, Julie. What did you learn about Julie?
5 In Unit 11 you listened to an interview about pandas. Seven reasons were given for the decline of the panda population. What were they?

b Compare your answers with two partners.

13 Looking after yourself

—— 1 ————————————————————————————

a In groups, discuss the following sentences. Decide whether they are True or False.

1 Coffee contains caffeine which stimulates the heart and nervous system and can cause headaches, diarrhoea and feelings of anxiety.
2 In the long term this can also lead to cancer and heart disease.
3 Tea is a much better substitute.
4 The best substitute is decaffeinated coffee.
5 Painkillers can also contain caffeine.

b Now read the following article to see if you are right.

Do you really need another cup of coffee?

Three or four cups of coffee a day may not sound excessive, yet some of the minor but debilitating symptoms many of us experience (like headaches, indigestion, palpitations) may be related to a quite modest caffeine intake.

A cup of 'real' coffee, percolated or filter, contains 100mg–150mg of caffeine, instant coffee, 80mg–100mg. Caffeine stimulates the nervous system, heart and kidneys and heavy coffee consumption (12 to 15 cups a day) is likely to produce signs of caffeine poisoning – headaches, irritability, buzzing in the ears, palpitations, indigestion, upset stomach and a general feeling of anxiety.

But even three or four cups, containing less than the daily recommended limit of 600mg, can also trigger one or more of these symptoms in susceptible people.

Dr Heather Ashton, Reader in Psychopharmacology at Newcastle-upon-Tyne Medical School, believes the effects that caffeine has also depend to some extent on personality and psychological factors. 'When treating people on tranquillisers, I have found that they are often sensitive to caffeine – it tends to make their symptoms worse. It seems likely that even a

Even a moderate intake can increase symptoms in people who are anxious

moderate caffeine intake can increase symptoms in people who are already anxious.'

The long-term health hazards of caffeine – such as cancer of the urinary tract, and breast and heart disease – have been the subject of much debate, but a large study carried out recently found no significant association between coffee consumption and any major cause of death.

It might be worthwhile, however, trying to find out if caffeine is responsible for some minor ills by gradually reducing intake. Switching to tea is not much help as a cup of tea can contain up to 100mg of caffeine. Cocoa and cola drinks also contain caffeine.

Decaffeinated coffee is not the answer either, because it tends to have greater gastrointestinal effects, sometimes causing indigestion or diarrhoea. And, like ordinary instant coffee, it also contains other substances (currently being researched) which may have undesirable effects on the nervous system.

Herbal teas, which contain low levels of caffeine, fruit juices and plenty of water are the best substitutes.

Also watch out for caffeine in painkillers and in cold remedies; you could end up ingesting several hundred milligrams of caffeine a day without even realising. Paracetamol or codeine are better, and cheaper, alternatives.

》》》→

c Practise the pronunciation of the following words. Where does the sound /aɪ/ (as in *side*) appear, and where does the sound /ɪ/ (as in *sit*) appear?

symptoms	diarrhoea	indigestion	antibiotics
hepatitis	disease	psychology	anxiety
constipation	diet	diabetes	virus

d Now listen to the cassette to check your answers.

e Complete the following sentences in a logical way and compare your answers with a partner.

1 You should go on a diet if ....

2 You often get indigestion if ....

3 A doctor may prescribe tranquillisers if ....

4 A doctor may prescribe antibiotics if ....

5 Diabetes is a disease caused ....

6 One of the symptoms of hay fever is ....

7 The best way to get rid of a headache is ....

8 If you get diarrhoea you should ....

───── **2** ─────────────────────────────

a The following lines describing the sequence of events in an illness are in the wrong order. Put them in the right order.

but fortunately I began to feel better after a day or so, ...

She seemed to think it was some kind of food poisoning. ....

I spent the next day in bed feeling absolutely dreadful, ...

Anyway, she gave me a prescription for some tablets and things ....

but I managed to get to the doctor's in the evening. ....

so I went home. I was sick all night. ....

At first they had little effect, ...

I started feeling funny at work on the Monday afternoon, ...*1*....

and eventually I went back to work on Friday. ....

and told me to take a couple of days off work. ....

b   With a partner write your own sequence of events for someone who has flu. Write the lines in the wrong order and see if another pair can put them in the correct order. You may need to use some of the following words:

a cough   a temperature   a sore throat   to start sneezing

— **3** —

a   If you remove a word from a text it is often possible to guess the missing word (or the general meaning of the word) from the context. For example, what is the missing word in the following examples, and how were you able to guess?

1   My hair was getting .... so I decided to get it cut.

2   I .... the bus so I had to take a taxi.

3   My hands were getting cold so I put on some ....

4   The rooms were very nice but the food was ....

5   I shut the door .... because I didn't want to disturb anyone.

b   Now try and guess the missing words in the following article, which is about the physical symptoms of panic. Before you read, think of some of the words and phrases you would expect to see in the text. Then read the article and look for clues to help you guess the missing words.

We're all likely to suffer from anxiety during our lives but the real problem starts when we can't .... it. DONNA DAWSON tells you how to...............

Panic can strike at any time. For example, the tube train suddenly .... in a tunnel. After a few minutes, Diane, 23, starts to .... After another minute, she feels a rising panic. She looks around, seeking silent reassurance from others, then tries to concentrate on her newspaper.

The train is still not moving. She starts to .... and her heart pounds in her ears; her breathing quickens, and her palms .... She strikes up a conversation with a complete .... – *anything* to try and calm herself. Just at the point where she feels she will physically lose control and start ...., the tube train starts to move. She is safe – until the next time.

What makes Diane so ....?

"It's to do with being closed in and unable to ....," she says. "I feel as though I can't breathe. I think of the worst that could happen – a fire, maybe – and I start to panic. What could I do? I'd probably run the wrong way. I feel that I'm not in control of the situation, and then I feel my body going out of control."

Diane has had this problem for a year now. She doesn't know how it ...., "it seemed to come out of the blue."

c   The actual words used in the article are in the box below. Complete the article using these words and then compare them with your first guess.

worry	stranger	anxious	get away	control	cope
sweat	shake	stops	screaming	started	

—— **4** ——————————————————————————

a Read through the following menu using the pictures to help you to identify new words.

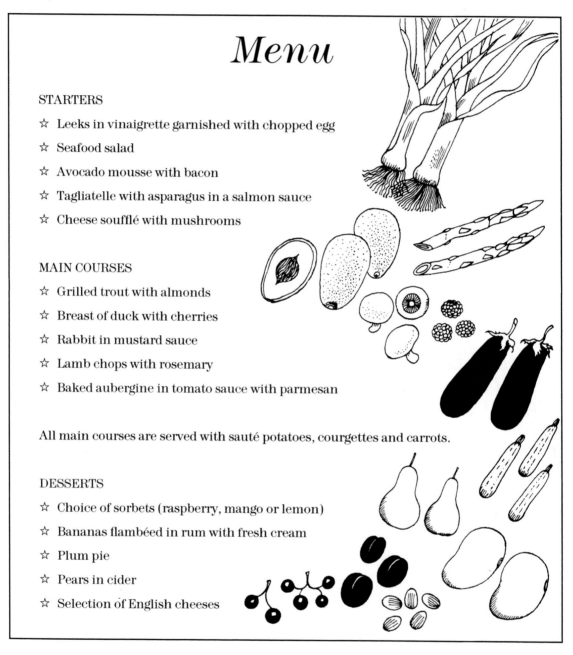

Menu

STARTERS

☆ Leeks in vinaigrette garnished with chopped egg

☆ Seafood salad

☆ Avocado mousse with bacon

☆ Tagliatelle with asparagus in a salmon sauce

☆ Cheese soufflé with mushrooms

MAIN COURSES

☆ Grilled trout with almonds

☆ Breast of duck with cherries

☆ Rabbit in mustard sauce

☆ Lamb chops with rosemary

☆ Baked aubergine in tomato sauce with parmesan

All main courses are served with sauté potatoes, courgettes and carrots.

DESSERTS

☆ Choice of sorbets (raspberry, mango or lemon)

☆ Bananas flambéed in rum with fresh cream

☆ Plum pie

☆ Pears in cider

☆ Selection of English cheeses

b   Listen to the conversation in which four people choose their meal from the menu. Which dishes in each course are *not* mentioned by any of the speakers?

c   **Now listen a second time and answer the questions below.**

1 One of the women doesn't want tagliatelle. Why not?
2 One of the men doesn't want seafood salad. Why not?
3 One of the men doesn't want rabbit. Why not?
4 One of the women doesn't want a meat or fish dish. Why not?
5 One of the men doesn't want plum pie. Why not?
6 One of the women doesn't want bananas. Why not?

d   **Imagine you are in a restaurant choosing a meal from the same menu. In groups of four, discuss and decide what each of you will have, and then give your order to your teacher.**

SELF-STUDY ACTIVITIES

1 Look back at the vocabulary network in Unit 12 (page 53), and then produce your own network around the word *illness*. Organise your network as you like, but consider the following:

  a) Examples of illness, e.g. hepatitis.
  b) Symptoms, e.g. a sore throat.
  c) Treatments, e.g. taking tablets.

2 We often borrow words from other languages, and in the menu opposite there are at least ten words that English has taken from other languages (including their pronunciation). Can you find them?
    Here are some more words used in English which have been taken from other languages. What do they mean and where do they come from?

chef	bureau de change	kindergarten	sauna	bidet
siesta	aperitif	duvet	elite	boutique	bon appetit

Think of some English words which are used in your first language. Are the words used in English with the same meaning?

3 Find a text in an English book and underline the new words as you read. Don't use a dictionary at this stage. When you have finished a section, go back and try to guess the exact meaning. Think about the part of speech, look at the words before and after, and think about the general idea that is being expressed. Use a dictionary to check your guesses.

14 Multi-word units

─── 1 ───

a How many words in the box can you use to complete each of the phrases on the left?

at the	front back top bottom beginning end	of the	....	
on the	front back	of the	....	
in the	middle	of the	....	
halfway	up down along through	the	....	

```
corridor
book
mountain
queue
list
page
plane
row
performance
course
meal
ladder
tunnel
unit
```

b Answer the following questions using prepositional phrases and nouns from **a**.

Example:

Where would you expect to find a pilot?   At the front of a plane.

1 Where would you normally find the toilets on a plane?
2 When do you have an interval?
3 Where would you find an index?
4 When do people often drink coffee and cognac?
5 Where do some people get claustrophobic?
6 When do some people get impatient and start pushing?
7 When would you usually take an exam?
8 When might some people get nervous?
9 When do you often have to stand up to let people get past?
10 Where can you find the title of this book?
11 Where can you find the Self-study activities?
12 Where can you find the Word-building tables?

—— **2** ——

a Read through the following dialogue. What are the two people talking about?

A: How many people turned up last night?
B: Just about everyone except for Tom.
A: Oh, what happened to him?
B: I've no idea. To tell you the truth, I haven't seen him for some time so I think he's more or less given up.
A: Well, that's a bit poor, isn't it? I mean, he's going to benefit as much as anyone when it's finished.
B: Oh yes, he's a great squash fan. Still, we'll just have to manage without him.
A: I guess so. How's it going anyway?
B: Well, generally speaking we're doing quite well. Up to now we've raised almost four thousand, and I'm hoping for another couple of hundred from my sponsored walk next week.
A: I thought Jill was doing that with you.
B: She was, but unfortunately she's done something to her back so I'll have to do it by myself.
A: Oh, that's a pity. Anyway, good luck – I hope it goes well.

b Replace parts of the dialogue in **a** with the following phrases. Work with a partner.

on the whole	apart from	so far	on my own	all the best
for quite a while	to be honest	what a shame	I suppose so	

c Make eight more changes to the dialogue. The meaning must stay the same. Work with a partner and, when you have finished, read your dialogue to another pair. Discuss any changes which you think are incorrect.

Example:
          came
A: How many people turned up last night?

—— **3** ——

a How many different prepositional phrases can you find by combining the prepositions on the left with the nouns on the right? Use a dictionary to check your answers.

in	strike	heart	business	fire	advance
by	mistake	time	choice	foot	chance
on					

b   Respond to the following questions using a suitable prepositional phrase in your answer. When you have finished, practise the dialogues with a partner.

Example:
A: Did you go by bus?
B: No, I went <u>on foot</u>.

1 A: Have they gone back to work?
   B: No, they're ....
2 A: Did you mean to take her coat?
   B: No, I ....
3 A: Did you have to take the exam?
   B: No, I ....
4 A: Did you give your speech from notes?
   B: No, I learnt ....
5 A: Were you planning to meet him?
   B: No, I ....
6 A: Is she there on holiday?
   B: No, she ....
7 A: Have the fire brigade put it out?
   B: No, it ....
8 A: Were you late for class this morning?
   B: No, I ....
9 A: Do you pay your rent at the end of the month?
   B: No, I ....

c   Can you think of any more prepositional phrases with *in, by* or *on*?

—— **4** ————————————————————

a   Write a sentence including the word *off* to describe what is happening or what has just happened in the following pictures.

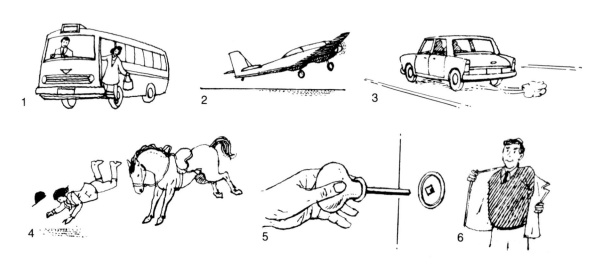

b   **What meaning (or meanings) does *off* have in the pictures in a?**

c   **Look at the following sentences. Is the meaning of *off* the same as above or different?**

1 When she saw me she hurried off in the opposite direction.
2 When are you off to Switzerland?
3 We didn't pay the bill so they cut off our electricity.
4 I went to the airport to see them off.
5 Follow the main road and turn off just before you get to the motorway.
6 I'm going to take a few days off work next week.

─────────────┤ **SELF-STUDY ACTIVITIES** ├────────────────────────────

1 New vocabulary often consists of two or more words, although each
   individual word may be familiar to you with a different meaning. For this
   reason, it is easy not to notice useful new phrases. So, when you are reading,
   pay careful attention to combinations of words. For example, can you find
   some useful multi-word verbs and phrases in the following short text?

Memo   To: ......Paul.................   Date: ...4.th June..............
         From: ...Alison...

I shall be off to Glasgow tomorrow for the conference. I'll be
away for at least a week but Mary has my number so you
can give me a ring if anything urgent comes up. I'll probably
call in at BPI on my way back to sort out the arrangements
for their next visit.

PS Could you try and fix up a meeting with Bill Stokes for
Tuesday week; he's usually tied up for weeks in advance but give
it a try.

2 Look at the eight sentences which include a verb + *on*. Find a suitable
   translation for each multi-word verb and then see if you can group them
   according to the meaning of *on*. (You did the same thing in Exercise **4**
   with *off*.)

   a) Could you turn on the tap?
   b) I tried on a couple of dresses in the shop.
   c) I got on the bus and then realised I'd left my money at home.
   d) I've worked hard in English but I'm not getting on very well.
   e) Several people tried to interrupt but I carried on talking.
   f) It was freezing cold so I put on my overcoat.
   g) I keep on getting a pain in my back.
   h) If this rain goes on much longer, the garden will be flooded.

15 Work

a Complete the chart below.

Job	Place	Duties
architect	office	designs buildings
		treats sick animals
	stock exchange	
fireman/woman		
	church	
dustman		
		operates on people
plumber		
	mine	
		writes newspaper reports
	library	
pilot		

b Now compile your own chart of the good and bad points of these jobs. Work with a partner and use a dictionary to help you. Example:

Job	Plus	Minus
pilot	well paid, exciting, high status	antisocial hours, stressful, early retirement

——— 2 ———

a Match ideas from column A with the information in column B.

A   *B*

company   on the outskirts of Manchester
career prospects   demanding but stimulating
salary   IBM
location   £30,000
responsibilities   comfortable and spacious offices
job satisfaction   company car and petrol allowance
fringe benefits   in charge of a small department
work environment   rapid promotion

b Rank the job factors in column A in order of importance to you personally and then compare your answers in groups.

——— 3 ———

Read the following article and complete the spaces with a suitable word. On page 67 you will find a box containing the missing words. Use this to help you if necessary.

JOBWATCH

Each week *Jean Robinson* investigates a trade or profession for the school leaver. This week she discovers what it is like to work as a Computer Programmer.

Susan Morley enjoys her work so much she also pursues it as a hobby.

As a Senior Computer Programmer for a leading credit card company she is .... for setting up data processing systems which handle the millions of transactions which take place every day all over the world between cardholders and retailers.

"This is the interesting bit," she laughingly told me.

"Checking whether the program is working correctly and producing the required information is repetitive and takes a great deal of concentration which is very ...."

Trainee

Susan was near the end of her 'A' level course when she .... to join the company as a trainee.

"I had no idea at this time what I wanted as a career, then I saw an .... in the local paper.

"I'm not brilliant, but you do have to be intelligent, logical and calm ..."

"The money seemed good, it didn't involve travelling to London every day and it didn't require me to spend long years studying."

Once in, Susan was given two months .... in programming language and systems analysis as well as other skills and general working methods of the company.

In the ever advancing world of computers it is necessary to be .... and willing to progress. As Susan said, "I'm not brilliant. I'd have gone into accounting if I had been, but you do have to be intelligent, logical and able to keep .... when everything is going wrong. Mistakes can be very expensive for the firm."

Susan is not too happy about her working environment at a desk in a large, noisy room which is badly lit and poorly ....

Privacy

There are other people working at desks all around her so there is little .... and it is difficult to concentrate.

"Personality is as important as practical skill in order to be able to get on with others," she explained.

"There are plenty of young people so it's easy to .... friends and there are excellent sports and social clubs to ...."

Susan works a 35 hour week and .... time enables her to start early in the morning and leave for home around 4.00pm. Besides a good .... structure there are other financial benefits such as cheap mortgages, personal loans and a Christmas ....

There is a profit sharing .... within the company and extra salary increases for good work.

Programmers with experience are in short supply which means good .... prospects with the corresponding salary increases.

4

a Recent research by an occupational psychologist has identified nine factors which contribute to happiness at work. They are:

1 The opportunity to exercise control
2 Variety
3 Security
4 Sufficient money
5 Decent working conditions
6 Friendships at work
7 The opportunity to use different skills
8 Demanding but not too demanding
9 A valued position in society

**Now look back at the article about Susan Morley.
How many of these nine points does her job provide?**

b How many of these qualities does your own job provide? Discuss in groups.

*'I've told you all about the pay,
holidays, hours, pension, sick pay,
perks and free lunches . . . wouldn't you
like to know what the job is?'*

---

1 In Unit 1 Exercise **4** you heard about the different ways in which a dictionary can help you. Look up the word *work* in a good monolingual dictionary and answer the following questions.

a) *Work* is a noun and a verb. Is it a countable or uncountable noun, or both? Is it a transitive or intransitive verb, or both?

b) Find three meanings/uses of *work* which are new to you but which seem useful. Copy the example sentences and try to add one of your own to each one. Try to use these meanings in the next few days.

c) Find three compounds or phrases with the word *work* and try to use them in the next few days.

d) Look at the phonemic script which shows you the pronunciation of the word *work*. Find five other words which have the same *vowel* sound.

e) Find another common word in the dictionary and investigate it in the same way.

2 Choose a job and then draw a network similar to the one below.

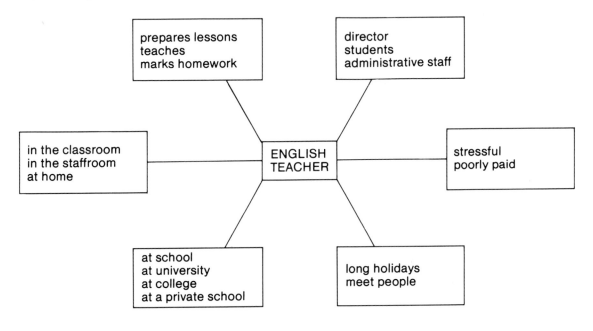

Here are the missing words from the article in Exercise **3**.

calm	responsible	training	scheme	privacy	adaptable
make	tiring	advertisement	salary	promotion	
join	ventilated	flexi-	bonus	applied	

16 Affixation 2

—— 1 ——

a Study the following word-building patterns and look up any new words:

Adjectives can be formed from nouns like this:

noun + -y e.g. dusty, hilly, healthy, touristy, sandy, dirty, chilly, rocky
noun + -al e.g. traditional, central, industrial, regional, commercial, seasonal
noun + -ic(al) e.g. economic/economical, symbolic, climatic, historic/historical, geographical, political

Verbs can be formed from nouns or adjectives like this:

noun / adjective + -ise e.g. modernise, industrialise, computerise, centralise, legalise, criticise

Notice the change in spelling in some of these examples, e.g. centre – central, industry – industrialise, history – historical.

b Prepare a short talk on one of the five subjects below and try to include as many words as possible from the list in **a**. You can use the root word or the derivative (i.e. *region* or *regional*, *modern* or *modernise*, etc.). When you are ready, give your talk to three other students. As you listen to the other students, make a note of the number of words they use from the list in **a**. Who has the most?

1 The climate in your country.
2 The major geographical features in your country.
3 The major industries in your country.
4 The major cities and distribution of population in your country.
5 A major social problem in your country.

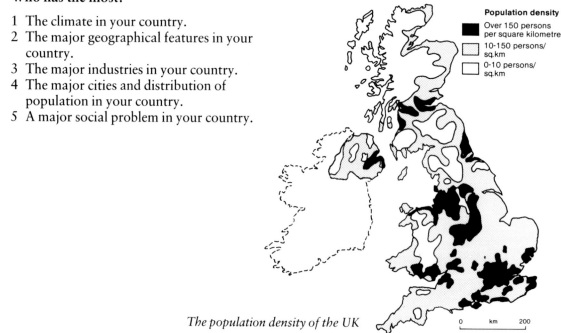

Population density

■ Over 150 persons per square kilometre
▨ 10-150 persons/ sq.km
□ 0-10 persons/ sq.km

The population density of the UK

0   km   200

──── 2 ────────────────────────────

a 🔲 Listen to the conversation on the cassette and write down all the words you hear which begin with the five prefixes below.

over-   de-   mis-   anti-   under-

When you have finished, discuss the meanings of these prefixes with your partner.

b Now think of other words which begin with these prefixes. Make sure the prefixes in your words have the same meaning as the examples from the cassette. (Use a dictionary if necessary.)

c 🔲 Listen to the conversation again. Can you find any more prefixes?

──── 3 ────────────────────────────

a We can form a number of verbs by adding '-en' to an adjective. Example:

soft + -en = to soften   sharp + -en = to sharpen
(Two common exceptions are *strengthen* and *lengthen*, where '-en' is added to the nouns *strength* and *length*.)

Reply to the following statements using a suitable verb ending with '-en':

Example:
A: This street is far too narrow for cars to overtake.
B: Yes, they ought to widen it.

1 A: This belt's a bit loose.
　B: ....

2 A: I think the trousers are too long.
　B: ....

3 A: I don't like my hair like this, it's too curly.
　B: ....

4 A: This sauce is too thin.
　B: ....

5 A: I think the strap is too short on this bag.
　B: ....

6 A: This knife is blunt.
　B: ....

7 A: I don't think the bridge is strong enough to take a lot of traffic.
　B: ....

———— 4 ————

a   You are going to read a passage about going down a coal mine. Before you read the passage, look at the picture and try to name some of the things you can see:

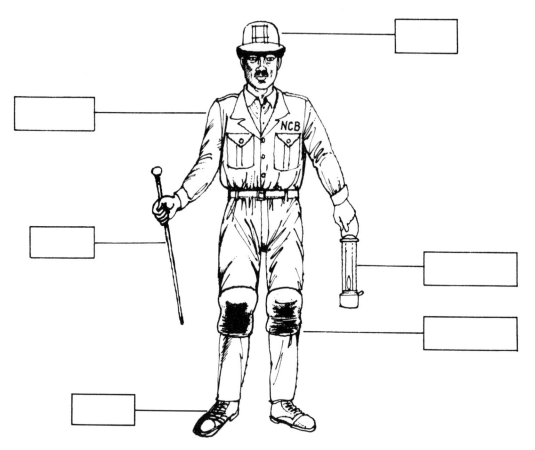

b   Now read the passage and finish labelling the picture in **a** with words from the passage:

The miner who took me down was a tallish man in his late thirties, dead white, thin and bony. He carried a Davy lamp and a stick with a carved round top, and he had a pair of black rubber pads round his knees. He was a deputy. 'A deputy,' he explained, 'deputises for the management in the pit. We are responsible at law for anything that goes wrong.' Later, talking about his job, he said, 'You won't find many people working in factories and other industries who are made responsible for so much. It's not an enviable position.'

   I was given a pair of overalls with 'N.C.B.' (National Coal Board) printed on them, and a white helmet.

There are probably quite a lot of words in this passage that you do not know. In **c** you will find some techniques to help you to guess the meanings of difficult words in a text *without* using a dictionary.

c The words in the list can all be divided into parts:

e.g. miner = mine + er

Divide the words into parts and think about their possible meanings:

miner   tallish   bony   enviable

The answer is that a *miner* is *someone who mines*. Which of the words in the box below follow a similar pattern?

higher	letter	farmer	deliver	drummer
murder	sweater	thriller	receiver	bitter
murderer	windscreen wiper		temper	finger

Tallish means *quite tall but not very tall*. **Which of the words in the box below follow a similar pattern?**

darkish	English	youngish	childish	rubbish
bluish	polish	yellowish	selfish	fish
twenty-sevenish		latish	finish	

Bony is an adjective related to the noun *bone*. **Which of the words in the box below follow a similar pattern?**

hairy	icy	heavy	pretty	salty	daisy
beauty	carry	daddy	story	woolly	cloudy
juicy	windy	sunny	silky	envy	

Enviable is an adjective which means *can be envied*. **Which of the words in the box below follow a similar pattern?**

reliable	noticeable	fashionable	variable
constable	comfortable	miserable	unbelievable
unrecognisable	unstable	reasonable	

| SELF-STUDY ACTIVITIES |
---

1 Look back at Exercise **1** of this unit and add two more examples to each of the four word-building patterns.

2 Many words in English can be used as a noun or a verb with no change in the form of the word, e.g. *a drink, to drink; a walk, to walk.* Sometimes the meaning stays the same, and sometimes it changes. Look at the examples below. Does the meaning change or stay the same? Use a dictionary to check your answers.

run	point	water	lead	gossip
dent	book	chair	dream	plant

3 Can you find two different meanings for the prefix 'dis-' in the words below? Divide the words into two groups according to these meanings.

dislike	disappear	disagree	disconnect
disobey	disloyal	disorganised	dishonest
disapprove	dissatisfied	dismount	disembark

17 Behaviour: People and verbs

— 1 —

a The sentences below all contain a mistake. They can be corrected in two ways:

a) by changing the underlined verb;
b) by keeping the verb but changing the rest of the sentence.

Correct the sentences in both ways.

Example:
She said me it was dangerous.
a) She told me it was dangerous.
b) She said (that) it was dangerous.

1 He entered into the building.
2 We were discussing about politics.
3 Could you explain me how this video works?
4 She wouldn't let me to go.
5 He made me to stay.
6 I've forgotten my books at home.
7 I'm waiting for a phone call this evening.
8 She suggested me to take an English course.
9 Could you remember me to turn off the central heating when we leave?

b Write a short story or dialogue of exactly 75 words (not 74 or 76) and try to include as many of the above verbs as possible (there are now 20). Work with a partner.

— 2 —

a Put the following sentences in order:

She might come. ....

She's bound to come. ....

She'll definitely come. ......_1_......

I doubt if she'll come. ....

She'll probably come. ....

She's highly unlikely to come. ....

She definitely won't come. ....

There's a fair chance that she'll come. ....

b   You are having a party this Friday. Read through the information below and discuss whether you think the different people will come to the party. Work in groups and use the language from **a**.

MICHAEL is a close friend of yours, he loves parties, and he has promised to bring some music cassettes. He used to go out with Jane.

MARIA is working until nine o'clock and her office is about ten miles from your house. She hasn't got a car, but she's an old friend.

BARBARA used to go out with Thomas but they split up a couple of weeks ago. At first she was very upset but she's beginning to get over it now.

THOMAS was the one who decided to end the relationship with Barbara, but he regrets it now and he's been very depressed.

BRIAN is working in Edinburgh until Thursday of this week, and then driving back down to London (400 miles) on Friday. He's very extrovert and sociable, although he can't stand Michael.

JANE has got exams starting on Monday, but she's not a very good student and doesn't think she'll pass. She is a good friend of Barbara's but she's also crazy about Thomas.

STEPHANIE is very shy, she loathes parties, and she often makes an excuse not to come to them. She said she would try to come but she may have to do overtime at work because her boss is away on holiday.

COLIN is not very keen on parties but he is mad about Jane and feels very protective towards her. He is also Barbara's cousin.

c   In actual fact, everybody went to the party and this is what happened:

Two people had a row.
Someone burst into tears and went home early.
Three people had a great time.
Someone got drunk and made a fool of themselves.
Someone turned up late and then fell asleep during the party.

Who did what and why?

—— 3 ——

a The following are all grammatically correct but one sentence in each group is a strange example. Find these strange examples and explain to a partner why they are strange.

1 She warned
   - them that the streets were dangerous late at night.
   - him not to go swimming near the rocks.
   - him that Maria was very beautiful.

2 They threatened
   - to go on strike.
   - to take me to a wonderful restaurant.
   - to kill the hostages.

3 She blamed
   - me for the accident.
   - John for making the party such a great success.
   - Peter for losing her pen.

4 I managed
   - to walk home, although it took me nearly five minutes.
   - to get there, despite losing my map.
   - to find a seat on the train, although it was in the rush hour.

5 He complained
   - about the food being overcooked.
   - to the police about the noise.
   - about the wonderful facilities at the new Sports Centre.

6 He denied
   - being my best friend.
   - stealing the typewriter.
   - that he was involved in the decision to sack the workers.

b With your partner think of situations in which the strange sentences above would be perfectly logical.

c Write your own sentence example for each of the six verbs. (Look carefully at the sentence construction in **a** to make sure the sentences are grammatically correct.) Then read your sentences to three other students. When all four have read their sentences, see how many examples each of you can remember.

'Satisfied? . . . I warned you not to invite the cows in for a few drinks.'

——— 4 ———

Complete the sequence of events in the four stories below. Try to use as many of the verbs in the box as you can.

apologise	resign	ignore	promise	blame
burst into tears	attack	go on strike	sack	offer
pretend	beg	threaten	swear (at)	
refuse	make (= force)		admit	

1 a) The workers asked for a 10% pay rise.
   b) The management offered them 5%.
   c) The workers turned down their offer.
   d) The management refused to increase their offer.
   e) The workers . . .

2 a) Anne complained about the amount of work she was given.
   b) Her boss ignored her complaint.
   c) Anne . . .
   d) Her boss . . .
   e) Anne . . .

3 a) Brian accused his wife of being unfaithful.
   b) She denied it.
   c) He . . .
   d) . . .
   e) . . .

4 a) Penny said the accident was Mike's fault.
   b) Mike . . .
   c) . . .
   d) . . .
   e) . . .

SELF-STUDY ACTIVITIES

---

1 This unit shows some of the constructions that are used with certain common verbs:

   a) Verb + full infinitive, e.g. *He refused to help.*
   b) Verb + object + full infinitive, e.g. *She told me to leave.*
   c) Verb + object + bare infinitive, e.g. *She made me work.*
   d) Verb + object + preposition, e.g. *He accused me of taking it.*
   e) Verb (to somebody) + preposition, e.g. *She apologised (to them) for being late.*
   f) Verb + (that) clause, e.g. *He said (that) we . . .*

   In which category (or categories) above do the following verbs belong?

manage	blame	remind	suggest
let	complain	promise	threaten
decide	warn	beg	force

2 This unit contains some common verbs which are used in special phrases, e.g. *make an excuse, fall asleep, burst into tears.* Here are six more you can learn.

   a) When I fell over everyone burst out laughing.
   b) He fell in love the moment he saw her.
   c) I tried to follow the instructions but they don't make sense.
   d) I'd like to go but I'm afraid I can't make it on Thursday.
   e) The car crashed into the wall and then burst into flames.
   f) I just opened the book and it fell apart.

18 Revision and expansion

In this unit you are going to revise vocabulary from Units 13 to 17, but you will also be learning some new vocabulary.

—— 1 ——

Write sentences with a verb + *on* or *off* which would produce the following replies.

Example:

A: Could you turn on the TV? → B: Yeah, sure. Which channel do you want?

1 A: .... → B: Oh, no. Was he badly injured?

2 A: .... → B: The next stop.

3 A: .... → B: Did it fit you all right?

4 A: .... → B: Well, that wasn't very polite, was it?

5 A: .... → B: Yes, of course. You can hang it up over there.

6 A: .... → B: Not very well, I'm afraid.

7 A: .... → B: Next Thursday.

8 A: .... → B: Well, some of these cheap radios are very badly made.

—— 2 ——

Organise the following words and phrases into meaningful groups. You must decide what the groups are and how many groups there are. Compare your answers with a partner when you have finished.

operate	scream	panic	promotion
ladder	put out	apply	symptoms
on fire	training	anxious	surgeon
suffer	sack	cancer	tremble
firemen	disease	apprentice	burst into flames
spread	scared	out of control	

3

a Find the adjectives formed from the nouns in the lists below. When you have finished, mark the stress on both the nouns and the adjectives. (You may need to use a dictionary.)

Noun	Adjective	Noun	Adjective
industry	industrial	commerce	
symbol		politics	
climate		economy	
history		allergy	
geography		finance	

b Now listen to the words on the cassette and check your answers.

c Can you find a rule for the position of the stress in adjectives with these endings? Are there any other adjectives which follow your rule?

4

a Complete the following grid to show the different ways that certain food can be cooked.

Cooking method / Food	fry	grill	boil	bake	roast	steam
eggs	✓	✗	✓	✓	✗	✗
aubergine						
duck						
salmon						
lamb chops						
cheese						

b Now produce your own grid for the following:

Cooking method / Food	wash	peel	chop	slice	eat raw	cook
ten different vegetables						

You could add more words (at the top or the side) if you think they are necessary.

───── **5** ──────────────────────────────────────

Write down the following:

1 Six verbs which are formed by an adjective + -en.
2 Six adjectives which are formed by a noun + -al.
3 Six verbs which are formed by a noun or adjective + -ise.
4 Ten adjectives which are formed by a noun + -y.

───── **6** ──────────────────────────────────────

Listen to the cassette and write down the sentences which you hear.

───── **7** ──────────────────────────────────────

Look at the example dialogue below and then write the other two dialogues
with a partner. When you have finished, read your dialogues to another pair.

1 A: *(Accusation)*   You were cheating in that exam, weren't you?
   B: *(Admission)*   Yes, I'm afraid I was.
   A: *(Threat)*   Well, if you do it again, you'll be thrown out of college.
   B: *(Promise)*   Don't worry. I'll never do it again.

2 A: *(Complaint)*   3 A: *(Accusation)*
   B: *(Apology)*   B: *(Denial)*
   A: *(Warning)*   A: *(Apology)*
   B: *(Promise)*   B: *(Threat)*

'Would you quit tapping your desk
with that pencil? . . .
I can't concentrate in here.'

8

a Complete the following sentences with the correct preposition.

1 You have to pay for the tickets .... advance.
2 She apologised .... being late.
3 He accused me .... stealing his pen.
4 She swore .... me.
5 I learnt the poem .... heart.
6 She's always complaining .... my food.
7 I'm not very keen .... tennis.
8 I should be able to cope .... this problem.
9 I live .... the outskirts .... Geneva.
10 She is responsible .... deliveries.

b Complete the following sentences in any way which is both logical and grammatically correct.

She

| denied .... |
| threatened .... |
| reminded .... |
| suggested .... |
| managed .... |
| explained .... |
| begged .... |
| ignored .... |
| warned .... |

9

How many phrases can you add to the following scale?

She'll definitely come. ←————————→ She definitely won't come.

10

a Find a prefix, a word or a phrase which you could use before each of the groups of words in column A. For column B, find a suffix, a word or a phrase which you could use after each of the groups of words.

A	B
.... manage / understand / lead	over / part / flexi ....
.... sleep / paid / weight	inflation / exchange / interest ....
.... loyal / honest / obey	tall / green / seven ....
.... freeze / social / septic	fly / hair / fresh air ....
.... tights / scissors / socks	friend / sponsor / apprentice ....

b Can you think of any more examples to add to any of these groups?

—— 11 ——

Rewrite each of the following sentences using a word from the list on the right. The meaning must not change.

Example:

That knife is too blunt.   sharp

That knife isn't sharp enough.

1 I don't have enough money to buy that car.   afford
2 She said it was my fault.   blame
3 He forced me to return the books.   make
4 I deal with marketing in my job.   involve
5 I'm sure she'll come.   bound
6 She let me go on my own.   allow
7 Does she own the flat?   belong
8 Don't panic!   calm

19 Right v. left

1

---

a Study the following sentences. Is there a single translation for *right* that you could use in your language?

1 Are you right-handed or left-handed?
2 Is the Democratic Party a right-wing party or a left-wing party?
3 I think you made the right decision.
4 I'm afraid I can't give you an answer right now, but I'll let you know tomorrow.
5 I tried to fix the TV but it's still not right.
6 Right, could I have your attention, please?
7 I think we have a right to know if the government keeps files on us.
8 Fill the bottle right to the top.

b Why do you think the word *right* often has a positive meaning? Does the word *left* have any negative meanings in your language?

2

---

a 🔲 Listen to the talk on the cassette and fill in the gaps.

1 The human ....

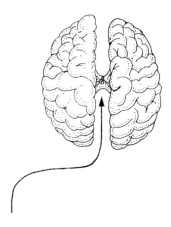

....

2 Linear ...., e.g. .... or ....

〉〉〉→

3 .... processing, e.g. .... or ....

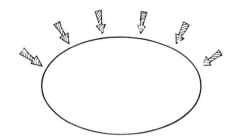

4

Left	Right
logical	....
rational	....
	....

b From your understanding of the recording, which will be the dominant side of the brain in the following human activities? Discuss with a partner.

1 Operating a computer
2 Making up stories
3 Bending your left leg
4 Working out mathematical
  problems
5 Moving your right thumb
6 Judging distances when driving

7 Recognising faces
8 Walking around without
  bumping into people
9 Typing
10 Marking an essay
11 Taking photos
12 Learning vocabulary

c And which side of the brain do you associate with the following adjectives?

methodical	romantic	emotional	idealistic	creative
realistic	analytical	impulsive	sceptical	

3

a Why can life be difficult for left-handed people? Discuss this with a partner for two or three minutes.

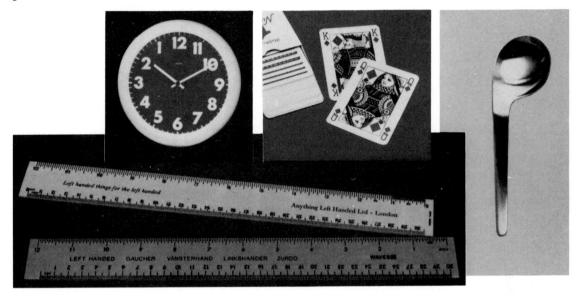

b Now read the following text and underline all the words and phrases which describe anger or unhappiness. Use a dictionary to check the meaning.

Are corkscrews and potato peelers a constant source of frustration? Do you feel like kicking cashpoint machines? Were you constantly in trouble at school for smudging your work? If so, you must be left-handed.

Approximately one in ten people are natural left-handers, and many of them resent living in a society which only seems to recognise right-handed people. It didn't stop famous 'lefties' such as Michelangelo, Alexander the Great, Joan of Arc and Picasso from achieving great things; but this is small comfort for the vast majority when simple tasks such as using a pair of scissors can be so irritating.

Now these people can join Left-Hand World – Britain's first national organisation for right thinking people who are proud to be left-handed. Derek Young, the brains behind the scheme, initially advertised the idea in several national newspapers; the response was amazing. Left-handers of all ages and backgrounds wrote to him with their own personal stories of suffering and humiliation. For many it was 'writing' which stirred the most painful memories. One man wrote, 'Even today, I can't bear the thought of picking up a pen.' And as recently as 30 years ago, teachers were tying children's left hands behind their backs, forcing them to write properly.

'Awful, but hardly surprising when you consider the prejudice around,' says Derek. 'The Bible makes it clear that God was right-handed and the Devil left-handed. Furthermore, the Latin word for left is "sinister", which means evil or threatening in English; the French word "gauche" means clumsy as well as left; and the Portuguese word "canhoto" can mean left, weak or mischievous.'

c   Complete the following sentences about yourself and then discuss them in groups.

1 I find it very frustrating when ....

2 I find it very irritating when ....

3 I resent ....

4 I can't bear the thought of ....

5 .... make(s) me very angry.

6 Children often suffer ....

7 I got into trouble ....

—— **4** ————————————————————————————

a *Left* and *Right* also represent positions on the political spectrum.

Left wing ←————————————————————————→ Right wing

Where would you place the following words on the scale above?

liberal	conservative	fascist	moderate
communist	socialist	reactionary	extreme

b   Answer the following questions and then compare your answers in groups.

1 Which political party is in power in your country?
2 How many major political parties are there in your country?
3 Do you elect the government in your country?
4 If so, how often do you have elections?
5 At what age can people vote in an election?
6 Is it compulsory to vote?
7 Can people vote if they are out of the country?
8 Can they vote if they are in prison?

c Political parties are often known under certain initials, e.g. CWP could stand for the Communist Workers' Party.

What could the following initials stand for?

CP   SLP   CDP   GP   SDLP   RWP   NFP

SELF-STUDY ACTIVITIES

1 In this unit we have seen that *left* and *right* are often used in opposition. What word is often used in opposition to each of the following?

public **private**   heaven
permanent   theory
fact   innocent
success   urban
profit   shortage

2 One way to record new words is by using a scale (as in Exercise **4**). Produce your own scales for the following:

a) always ⟵————————————⟶ never
b) love   ⟵————————————⟶ hate
c) boiling ⟵————————————⟶ freezing (weather)

3 Here are some common initials used in English. What do they stand for?

BBC   UN   p.m.   NATO   EC   DIY   MP   PM

20 Ways of looking at things

—— 1 ——

a Label the numbered parts and objects below using the words on the right. You will need to use some words more than once.

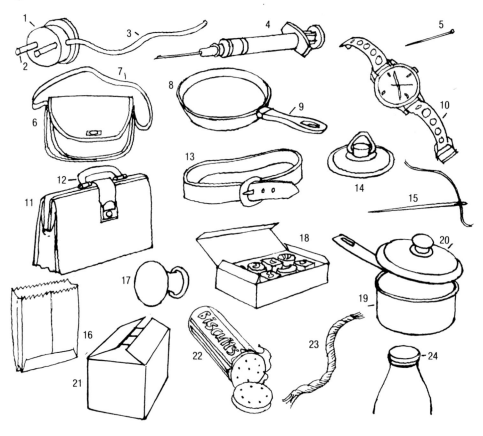

belt
plug
handle
top
lid
needle
rope
box
packet
bag
briefcase
strap
pin
frying pan
saucepan
lead

b How many different words would you need in your own language to label the numbered parts and objects above? If possible, compare your answer with someone who speaks a different language.

c Draw the following objects and see if a partner can identify each one. Use a dictionary to help you if necessary.

1 a pin and a nail
2 a bag and a basket
3 a bush and a hedge
4 fingers and toes
5 a comb and a brush

6 steps and stairs
7 a jug and a jar
8 a bowl and a vase
9 a piece of rope and a piece of string

88

—— 2 ——

a It is sometimes easier to remember a word if you connect it with a particular image or association. Try the following examples. Read through the list slowly, using a dictionary to check the meaning of new words.*

A ladder can be used as a bookshelf.
A leaf can be used as a bookmark.
A newspaper can be used to kill flies.
A knife can be used to stir paint.
Scissors can be used to cut grass.
A balloon can be used as a pillow.
A bottle can be used as a vase.
A coin can be used as a screwdriver.
A sheet can be used as a sail.
The edge of a book can be used as a ruler.

b Now cover the right-hand words and read through the nouns on the left. Do they help you to remember the words on the right?

c Try making your own associations for the words below. When you have finished, read your associations to a partner and see if he or she can tell you the word you are describing.

| a brick | a comb | a stick | an umbrella |
| a bucket | a scarf | a spoon | a diamond |

*Exercise **2** is based on an experiment quoted in *Human Cognition* by J. Bransford, Wadsworth Inc., 1979.

—— 3 ——

a Look at the different pictures of Muriel Gray and complete the following sentences. Compare your answers in groups.

1 She looks very .... in picture ....
2 Picture .... makes her look ....
3 In picture .... she looks as if she's ....
4 She looks like a .... in picture ....
5 I think picture .... is definitely the best.

b The following sentences are Muriel Gray's own opinions about the pictures. Try to match the sentences with the pictures, and decide what fee she was charged for each picture – the different fees are in the box.

1 'A perfectly decent and acceptable caricature. If anything, slightly flattering and not critical enough. The eyes could be piggier.'

2 'I will never be exactly glamorous but in this photo at least I look human.'

3 'This looks like someone who is mentally ill, but then I am rarely told to smile. If I want the puppy's picture taken I know where to go.'

4 'It resembles a police artist's impression of someone they are looking for in connection with the mugging of old age pensioners.'

5 'I had a major identity crisis when I first saw this picture. Even though I'm looking at the photographer with contempt I still look like a stupid tart.'

6 'It's not ugly enough. My mouth is tiny and mean, not horsey and generous like this. The clothes are all wrong too. My style, if you can call it that, is plain and simple; I possess no wild blouses.'

7 'I don't believe it's possible to look even remotely pleasant in one of these pictures, so the best policy is to pull a face.'

8 'A shy young artist who is swept off her feet by a passionate Italian gallery owner. I don't look like this.'

9 'I can see a filling that needs seeing to.'

£425	£1	£275	£10	£3,000
£750	£42	£1,500	£130	

SELF-STUDY ACTIVITIES

1 In Exercise **3a** you used a number of different constructions with the verb
  look. Now write four sentences for each of the verbs below using the same
  constructions.

  taste   feel   sound   smell

  Example:
  This soup tastes strange.
  She sounds as if she's got a cold.

2 At home find six objects which you can draw, and then use a bilingual
  dictionary to find the names of these objects in English. In your next lesson,
  draw the six objects for a partner and see if they can identify each one in
  English. If not, teach them the words.

3 There are lots of ways of looking at things – it depends what you are looking
  at. Which of the things in the left-hand box would you use to look at the things
  in the right-hand box?

dark glasses	a magnifying glass
binoculars	opera glasses
a telescope	a wide-angle lens
spectacles	a microscope

a play	a beetle
a planet	a rare bird
the television	bacteria
a sunny beach	
a large group of people	

21 Problems

a In this unit you will look at several problems. There are many things you can do to a problem: you can . . .

cause it	ignore it	do something about it	solve it	face it
anticipate it	tackle it	make it worse	reduce it	

Use a dictionary to look up the meanings of any new words.

b Read the following statements. In groups, discuss what the problem might be in each case, and whether you agree with the statements.

1 It wouldn't solve the problem completely but if more people left their cars at home, at least it would reduce it.
2 I think it's the duty of Western governments to do something about it, otherwise millions could die through no fault of their own.
3 Some people say it's a problem that only doctors and scientists can tackle, but I think it's a simple question of education.
4 I don't think anyone anticipated the potential problems when they were first developed; if they had, the world would be a much better place to live in.
5 You often get a few funny squeaks and rattles, but if you ignore them, they usually go away.
6 It's no good telling him – it'll only make it worse. There are some things we have to learn for ourselves.

Which of the following adjectives would you use to describe each of the problems above?

serious	urgent	minor	exaggerated	delicate
long term	complex	common	social	

a The following words are from three different newspaper stories. What are the three stories? Group the words according to which story they belong to. (You can use the same word in more than one story.) Use a dictionary to help you.

survivors	aid	fish	conservationists	buried	leak
polluted	trapped	drought	Ethiopia	industrial waste	
chemical plant		starving	debris	crop failure	furious
save	escape	famine	earthquake	poisoned	collapsed

b Here is one of the stories. Fill in the gaps with words from **a**.

Hundreds are feared dead after an .... in the small Turkish town of Varto. Most of the victims were .... beneath tons of rubble and ...., as shops and offices .... on top of them. Rescue workers have so far recovered nearly 80 bodies but the final death toll could be three or four times that number.

The worst hit area was the central business district. Many shop and office workers were making their way to lunchtime bars and restaurants when the tremors started. Most of those in the street managed to .... but many more were .... inside buildings as ceilings fell in and falling masonry blocked exits. Rescue workers are continuing the search for ...., and the army is sending in more troops to help with the rescue operation.

c Now join the words below into another short newspaper story.

Conservationists . . . furious . . . a leak . . . a chemical plant . . . industrial waste . . . polluted . . . rivers . . . poisoned . . . fish . . .

——— 3 ———

a Make sure you understand the meaning of the following words and phrases. Work with a partner and use a dictionary to help you. Can you organise the words and phrases in a more helpful way?

a riot	shoplifting	commit a crime
remand somebody in custody	revenge	punish
release somebody	court	reform
convict somebody of a crime	a minor offence	prison sentence
a serious offence	on parole	trial

b ▭ Listen to the conversation on the tape about overcrowding in prisons. What four suggestions are made to help to solve this problem?

c What do you think? Discuss the question in groups.

——— 4 ———

a Choose an adjective from the box on the right to describe each of the actions in the box on the left. (If none of the adjectives are suitable, find another.)

People who . . .   *are . . .*

1 leave lights on
2 play loud music
3 park illegally
4 drop litter
5 leave taps running
6 spend money on things they don't need
7 throw away good food
8 demand higher salaries all the time
9 push in front of people in queues
10 buy all their food in supermarkets
11 drive instead of walking, cycling or using public transport

thoughtless
lazy
selfish
greedy
impatient
materialistic
practical
sensible

b Do you do any of these things? Choose *one* that you do, and *one* which makes you angry. Move around the class and discuss your answers with other students.

Example:
I often leave lights on in the house and waste electricity. The thing that makes me angry is people who push in front of me in queues. What about you?

》》》→

C In groups, discuss which of the actions might *cause, lead to* or *contribute to* the following problems:

traffic congestion   floods   pollution   poverty   famine
stress   rising crime rates   unemployment

SELF-STUDY ACTIVITIES
---

1 The verbs below have all appeared in this unit. Using a dictionary if necessary, find the nouns formed from these verbs.

Verb	*Noun*	*Verb*	*Noun*
contribute	contribution	convict	
anticipate		punish	
cause		fine	
bury			

2 Imagine you are a journalist reporting from Ethiopia. Write a short report (approximately 120 words) on the situation in Ethiopia. (Use vocabulary from Exercise **2**.)

3 Complete the problems on the left with the mixed up explanations on the right.

It won't open –	it's run out of gas.
It won't start –	it's jammed.
I can't work it out –	it's too complicated.
It won't light –	it's too dark in here.
I can't get it on –	the battery's flat.
I can't make it out –	it isn't my size.

22 Connecting words and ideas 2

a Vocabulary plays an important part in shaping and developing a conversation. Look at the following examples:

A: I thought the play was awful.
B: Oh, come on, it wasn't that bad.

A: Their new flat is tiny.
B: I don't know . . . it isn't that small.

Reply to the following statements using a suitable adjective in each case.

1 The garden is huge.
2 Their new album is brilliant.
3 He was absolutely furious.
4 I thought the film was hilarious.
5 The weather was dreadful.
6 This room is absolutely freezing.
7 The hotel costs a fortune.
8 The beach was packed yesterday.

b Vocabulary can continue to play a part in connecting the ideas as the conversation develops. Look at these examples:

A: I thought the play was awful.
B: Oh, come on, it wasn't that bad.
A: Yes, it was. Some of the acting was dreadful.
B: Yeah, perhaps, but the main characters were OK.

A: Their new flat is tiny.
B: I don't know . . . it isn't that small.
A: Yes, it is. You can hardly turn round in the kitchen.
B: Yes, I know, but the lounge is a reasonable size.

With a partner, develop and practise similar conversations for three examples from 1–8 in a.

——— **2** ———————————————————————————————

a Choose phrases from the columns to complete this sentence.

You ought to buy an umbrella . . .

otherwise . . .	you get there.
unless . . .	the weather's nice at the moment.
once . . .	you don't get wet if it rains.
as . . .	you haven't got a raincoat.
in case . . .	carry a raincoat around with you.
rather than . . .	the weather improves.
so that . . .	you might get wet.
even though . . .	it rains.

b Now complete the following sentences in a suitable way.

I think you should change some traveller's cheques . . .

in case ....
unless ....
otherwise ....
so that ....
even though ....
as ....
rather than ....
once ....

——— **3** ———————————————————————————————

a In Unit 8, Exercise **2** showed how synonyms are often used to organise and develop a text. The same is true of antonyms.

Examples:
I thought the exam would be <u>easy</u>, but in actual fact it was quite <u>tricky</u>.
One minute he <u>admits</u> he made a mistake, the next minute he <u>denies</u> it.

The presence of opposites is another way to help you to guess the meaning of unknown words. In the first example above, *easy* helps you to guess that *tricky* means *difficult*.

b Find the words and phrases which are being used in opposition in the following texts. See if the opposition helps you to guess the meaning of unknown words and phrases.

When you're tense they relax you, when you're tired they wake you up.

I'm afraid most of this essay is irrelevant. You must learn to keep to the point.

Spend a day in Milton Keynes. And as you travel back to your cramped London office, through traffic lights, traffic jams and pollution, think about the city you've just left: a city carefully concealed by the surrounding countryside, with uncongested roads, open spaces, and clean air.

Overall, I think I'm still the one who plays safe, the down-to-earth one. Jane is a great risk-taker, but she is much better at keeping her cool, even in the midst of chaos.

I know what it's like to be broke; and I know what it's like to have everything you want.

The arrangement is due to expire in May next year unless the two countries agree by November 14 to prolong it.

c   Complete the following text with suitable words or phrases. When you have finished, compare your answers with the words and phrases in the box on page 100.

The house looks marvellous now but it was very .... when we bought it three years ago. The problem with old properties is that they require constant attention; sadly, however, the previous owners .... the place for years and it was badly in need of renovation.

At first we planned to do up the house ourselves. Unfortunately, that idea proved to be rather unrealistic and, ..., we had to bring in builders for some of the difficult jobs. The back extension which included the kitchen, for example, was so dangerous that we had to have it .... and rebuilt.

The changes we made also produced some terrible rows. I wanted to keep the old enamel bath which I thought was rather attractive; Mary, on the other hand, was determined to .... it and install a modern shower cubicle. We argued about it for ages but finally reached a .... to keep the bath and install a shower.

It wasn't all misery, though. We got a great deal of .... from seeing a derelict shell gradually being transformed into a ....; and for a person like myself who has always preferred to play safe, it was very exciting to do something a bit .... for a change.

d **Look through the completed text again and see how many examples of synonymy you can find.**

Example:
house   property   place

SELF-STUDY ACTIVITIES

1 Take four texts from an English newspaper (or from a coursebook) and see how many examples of antonymy you can find.

2 Use as many of the link words as you can from Exercise **2** to complete the following sentences in different ways:

I booked a table for six ....

I did my homework last night ....

You should get the job ....

3 a) In Exercise **3c** of this unit you saw how synonymy and antonymy help to organise and develop the ideas in a text. From this we get a group of words all about house improvements:

home   property   place   residence
run-down   in need of renovation   derelict
do up   renovate
knock down   rebuild
bath   shower
owner   builder
install   get rid of
back extension

Can you add any more likely words and phrases to this group?

   b) Choose a text on a particular topic. Read the text and build your own lexical set around the topic.

Here is the box to help with Exercise 3c:

compromise	beautiful residence	risky
run-down	pleasure	knock down
neglect	get rid of	in the end

23 Night and day

1

a There are a number of compound words or phrases containing *day* or *night*. Look at the lists below. Is the missing word *day* or *night* or could it be either of them?

.... shift   ....dream   over..................
one of these ....   last ....   the other ....
..................club   ....life   the .... before yesterday
.... return   good..................   the .... before last
.... watchman   ....dress

b Transfer the above words and phrases to this network.

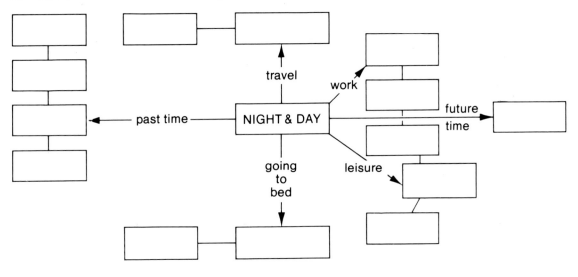

2

a Organise the following words and phrases into groups. You must decide what the groups are and how many groups there are. Work with a partner and compare your answers with another pair when you have finished.

sleeping pills	fall asleep	go for a walk
dream	count sheep	go to bed
get up	wake up	insomnia
have a nightmare	sleepwalk	sleep like a log
do exercises	snore	have a restless night
be fast asleep	have a nap	awake

101

b Move round the class interviewing other students. Try to find someone who . . .

1 used to sleepwalk as a child
2 has a recurrent nightmare
3 does exercises either before they go to bed or immediately after they wake up
4 finds it difficult to sleep in a strange bed
5 can fall asleep easily when travelling on a coach, train or plane
6 never takes sleeping pills
7 enjoys having a nap during the day
8 likes a hard bed and someone who likes a soft one
9 suffers from insomnia
10 snores a lot

———— **3** ————

a Why do some people work at night? With a partner, make a list of the advantages and disadvantages of working nights.

b 🖭 Listen to the conversation on the cassette, and add any advantages or disadvantages that were not in your list.

c What do the following words mean, and in what connection are they used in the conversation? If necessary, listen to the cassette again.

jet lag	a vicious circle	thick curtains	masks
ruin (your social life)	statistically	an owl or a fox	

d *Get* is a very common verb in spoken English because it can be used with a number of different meanings. What is the meaning of *get* in the following sentences from the conversation?

1 I don't think you ever get used to it really.
2 It's the people who can't get work during the daytime who work the night shifts.
3 There are problems with both the quantity of sleep they get and the quality.
4 Actually that's one of the advantages, if you've got kids at school, that you can be there when they get home from school.
5 But you get normal weekends?

——— 4 ———

a Here are some short excerpts from novels in English. Read each one and decide at what time of day each one takes place. You should use a dictionary but do not try to understand every word. Underline the words which helped you to guess the time of day or night.

1 The sky was a grey wash; pale grey over the fields behind the estate, but darkening overhead, to charcoal away over the city. The street lamps were still on and a few lighted windows glowed the colours of their curtains. Billy passed two miners returning silently from the night shift.   (*Kes* by Barry Hines)

2 When he awoke the hawk was back on the pole and the sun was directly above the farm.   (*Kes* by Barry Hines)

3 A few yards along the path, and the houses had faded from dull red to dark shapes in the dusk. Only the silhouette of their roofs showed clearly against the sky.   (*Kes* by Barry Hines)

4 A shadow rippling across a drawn curtain. A light going on. A light going off. A laugh. A shout. A name. A television on too loud, throwing the dialogue out into the garden. A record, a radio playing; occasional sounds on quiet streets.   (*Kes* by Barry Hines)

5 The station was ablaze with cold, white light. The booking hall was deserted except for a fleet of electric trollies piled high with news-paper parcels. The last Harrogate diesel was just pulling sleekly away from platform two. The inquiry office was closed.
                           (*Billy Liar* by Keith Waterhouse)

6 When the grave was nearly deep enough, he went back to the car for the carpet. But now, it was much brighter, and the sun was touching the tops of the trees.
                (*A Suspension of Mercy* by Patricia Highsmith)

7 House roofs were flushed orange by the setting sun, and a green luminous light crossed the house walls of the opposite terrace.
                (*Saturday Night, Sunday Morning* by Alan Sillitoe)

8 The sun was not yet up, and the lawn was speckled with daisies that were fast asleep. There was dew everywhere. The grass below my window, the hedge around it, the rusty paling wire beyond that, and the big outer field were each touched with a delicate, wandering mist.
                       (*The Country Girls* by Edna O'Brien)

b Now write one or two sentences describing a scene and see if your partner can guess the time of day.

┤ **SELF-STUDY ACTIVITIES** ├

1 Look back at Unit 1 Exercise **2b**. Try to use most of the same expressions to explain the following words and phrases. In your next lesson test another student with your explanations.

nightie	fortnight	nightingale	nightcap
weekday	daybreak	day nursery	pay day
a week today	night watchman		

2 Study the word-building tables at the back of the book and prepare a short test of ten questions for your partner in the next lesson.

Examples:
What's the opposite of *asleep*?
What noun is formed from the verb *inherit*?
What preposition follows the adjective *critical*?

3 Find one preposition which would fit into *all* the following sentences.

a) .... times I wanted to kill him.
b) You shouldn't go out alone late .... night.
c) .... least nobody got hurt.
d) She's hard .... work mending the car.
e) Somebody threw a bottle .... the goalkeeper.
f) Her grandfather died .... 97.
g) I'm absolutely terrible .... parking.
h) The children all grinned .... each other.
i) Tell him I can see him .... noon .... the earliest.
j) The plane left the ground .... about 200 m.p.h.

4 In your language could you use *one* word in all the sentences above? If not, concentrate on the differences between your language and English.

24 Revision and expansion

In this unit you are going to revise vocabulary from Units 19 to 23, but you will also be learning some new vocabulary.

1

Look at the following pictures.

pear

turn on

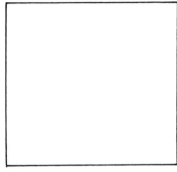

even

It is easy to show the meaning of *pear* in a picture; *turn on* is more difficult but still possible; *even* is impossible, and that is why there is no picture. Divide the words in the box below into three similar groups. Draw the words which are in the first group, and think about the pictures you would need to explain words in the second group. Work with a partner.

ban	fence	ceiling	mean (adj.)	stir	unless
fall asleep	string	rarely	on purpose	ruler	
pick (something) up	resemble		pull a face	notorious	

2

Combine phrases from the following three columns to form logical sentences, and then put the sentences in the correct chronological order.

A	B	C
She was tried	to ten years in prison	at the police station.
She was arrested	of manslaughter	by the jury.
She was sentenced	outside her house	in the High Court.
She was convicted	with manslaughter	by the judge.
She was charged	for manslaughter	by plain-clothes police officers.

3
---

a The words below are all two-syllable verbs with the stress on the second syllable. For each one find two other verbs which rhyme with the second syllable.

Example:
re<u>pair</u>   despair   compare

re<u>duce</u>   re<u>ply</u>   re<u>tain</u>   re<u>form</u>   re<u>spect</u>   re<u>mand</u>

b 🔲 Listen to the cassette and check your answers. Write down any words from the recording which are not on your list.

4

Complete the following sentences with suitable link words.

1 .... it was raining, I decided to stay at home.
2 .... it was raining, I decided to go out.
3 You'd better take the extra money .... you have to take a taxi.
4 I'd better go now, ... I'll miss my bus.
5 .... I go now, I'll miss my bus.
6 I took my Walkman .... I could listen to music on the train.
7 It seems difficult at first, but .... you get the hang of it, operating a
   computer is quite easy.

5
---

a Mark the stress on the nouns below and then complete the right-hand columns.

Noun	Verb	Noun	Verb
de<u>cision</u>	decide	anticipation	
solution		pollution	
imagination		reduction	
competition		explosion	
persuasion		recognition	

b 🔲 Listen to the cassette and check your answers.

6

Name the following objects and then rearrange them in order from the
lightest to the heaviest. Work with a partner.

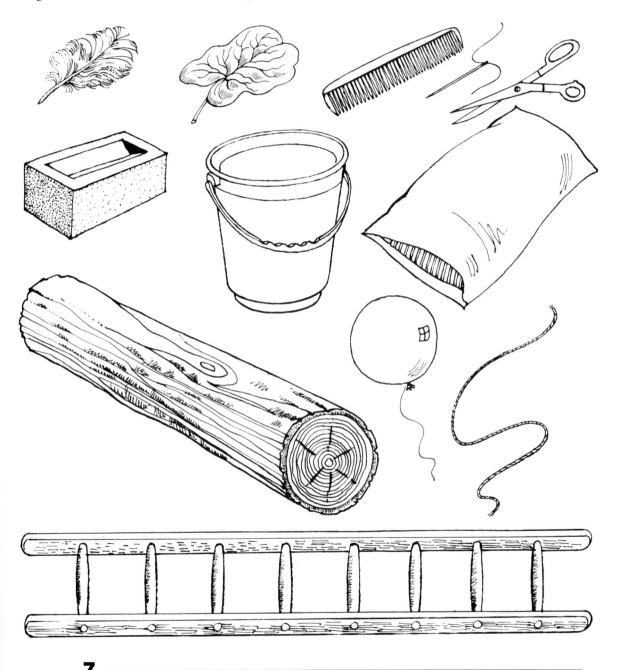

7

Listen to the ten sentences on the cassette. Write down each one as you
listen and then check your answers with a partner.

—— **8** ——

a Study the adverbs and adjectives below. Can you find a general rule for the use of these adverbs with adjectives?

Adverb	Adjective	Adverb	Adjective
absolutely	packed	very	good
	huge	extremely	interesting
	fascinating	incredibly	big
	exhausted		small
	brilliant		boring
	dreadful		upset

b Which of the above adverbs could you use with the following adjectives?

funny	hilarious	cold	chilly	unique	bitter
impossible	angry	furious	crowded	freezing	tiny
confused	tolerant	restless	sensitive	nice	

—— **9** ——

Write a story using the framework below. Your story can be as long or short as you like, and in any order you like, but all the expressions must be there.

You'll never guess what happened to me the other day. I was
.... when all of a sudden
....
At first I thought ...., but then I realised
....
Anyway, ...
Fortunately, (or Unfortunately), ..., so ....
Eventually, ...

—— **10** ——

Look at the following. Do you think these people would be left- or right-brain oriented? Discuss in groups and give reasons for your answers. (Look again at Unit 19 Exercise **2** if you need help.)

doctors	lawyers	tax experts	bookkeepers
poets	musicians	writers	top executives
politicians	dancers	architects	

Word-building tables

Building new words from the 'root' form is an important part of vocabulary expansion. For example, to the verb *improve* we can add the suffix *-ment* to form the noun *improvement*; to the noun *topic* we can add *-al* and form the adjective *topical*. Sometimes there will be a small change in spelling, e.g. the noun from *organise* is *organisation* (not *organiseation*).

There are no clear rules about the use of suffixes in word building, but some suffixes are very common and you can sometimes guess the correct suffix to build a new word. Here are some common examples – see how many words you can think of with these suffixes and then check your words in the tables on the following pages.

Noun (abstract)	Noun (person)	Adjective	Verb
-tion	-er	-ent	-ise
-sion	-or	-al	
-ment	-ian	-y	
-y		-ous	
-ness		-able	
-ity		-ive	

All of the words in these tables are presented in the book in at least *one* form. Some of the forms, however, will be new to you, and they must be learned. With regular study this is a quick and easy way to expand your vocabulary.

—————— | **TABLE 1: General noun + personal noun + adjective + verb** | ——————

General noun	Personal noun	Adjective	Verb
aggression	aggressor	aggressive	
analysis	analyst	analytical	analyse
application	applicant		apply (for)
architecture	architect	architectural	(design)
art	artist	artistic	(paint)
attack	attacker		attack
communism	communist	communist	
competition	competitor	competitive	compete
conservation	conservationist		conserve
conservatism	conservative	conservative	
criticism	critic	critical (of)	criticise
defence	defender	defensive	defend
democracy	democrat	democratic	democratise
diabetes	diabetic		
economy/economics	economist	(un)economic/al	economise
(un)employment	employee/er	(un)employed	employ
extremism	extremist	extreme	
fascism	fascist	fascist	
finance	financier	financial	finance
geography	geographer	geographical	
hijacking	hijacker	hijacked	hijack
history	historian	historical	
hunting	hunter		hunt
idealism	idealist	idealistic	idealise
industry	industrialist	industrial	industrialise
insomnia	insomniac		
invention	inventor	inventive	invent
investigation	investigator	investigative	investigate
investment	investor		invest
kidnap/ping	kidnapper		kidnap
liberalism	liberal	liberal	
management	manager	managerial	manage
mathematics	mathematician	mathematical	
moderation	moderate	moderate	
music	musician	musical	(compose)
organisation	organiser	(dis)organised	organise
performance	performer		perform
photography	photographer	photographic	photograph
politics	politician	political	politicise
practice	practitioner	(im)practical	practise
product/production	producer	(un)productive	produce
reality/realism	realist	(un)real/istic	realise
science	scientist	(un)scientific	
socialism	socialist	socialist	
survival	survivor		survive

(Table 1 continued)

General noun	Personal noun	Adjective	Verb
symbol	symbol	symbolic	symbolise
terrorism	terrorist	terrorist	terrorise
election	the electorate	electoral	elect
theory	theorist	theoretical	theorise
theft	thief		(steal)
use	user	useful/less	use

───── **TABLE 2: Noun + verb** ────────────────────────────────

Noun	Verb	Noun	Verb
accusation	accuse	punishment	punish
admission	admit	recovery	recover
agreement	agree (with)	reduction	reduce
anticipation	anticipate	refusal	refuse
(dis)appearance	(dis)appear	relief	relieve
argument	argue	renovation	renovate
burial	bury	requirement	require
calculation	calculate	resemblance	resemble
cancellation	cancel	reservation	reserve
choice	choose	resignation	resign
comparison	compare (sthg. with sthg.)	restriction	restrict
complaint	complain	revision	revise
confirmation	confirm	solution	solve
connection	connect	starvation	starve
conviction	convict (sb. of sthg.)	storage	store
delivery	deliver	suffering	suffer
denial	deny	suggestion	suggest
discovery	discover	threat	threaten
discussion	discuss	treatment	treat
distinction	distinguish (between)	trial	try (sb. for sthg.)
entrance	enter	(mis)understanding	(mis)understand
exaggeration	exaggerate	warning	warn
expiry	expire	wreckage	wreck
explosion	explode		
failure	fail		
identification	identify		
improvement	improve		
inheritance	inherit		
installation	install		
judgement	judge		
pollution	pollute		
postponement	postpone		
prescription	prescribe		
preservation	preserve		

TABLE 3: Noun + adjective

OPP. = Opposites which we feel are sufficiently common or useful to include.

Noun	Adjective	Noun	Adjective
agility	agile OPP. clumsy	risk	risky OPP. safe
allergy	allergic	rock	rocky
anger	angry	salt	salty
anxiety	anxious	sand	sandy
hill	hilly OPP. flat	season	seasonal
bone	bony	space	spacious OPP. cramped
chaos	chaotic OPP. organised	sun	sunny
chill	chilly OPP. warm	tension	tense OPP. relaxed
climate	climatic	tourist	touristy OPP. unspoilt
cloud	cloudy	tradition	traditional
comfort	(un)comfortable	tragedy	tragic
commerce	commercial	ugliness	ugly OPP. beautiful
complexity	complex OPP. simple	urgency	urgent
cruelty	cruel OPP. kind	wind	windy
darkness	dark		
dirt	dirty OPP. clean		
dust	dusty		
effect	(in)effective		
efficiency	(in)efficient		
elegance	elegant		
emotion	(un)emotional		
extinction	extinct		
fashion	(un)fashionable		
flexibility	(in)flexible		
fog	foggy		
formality	(in)formal		
fury	furious		
generosity	generous OPP. mean		
glamour	glamorous		
grammar	(un)grammatical		
guilt	guilty OPP. innocent		
hunger	hungry		
ice	icy		
innocence	innocent OPP. guilty		
juice	juicy OPP. dry		
kindness	(un)kind		
logic	(il)logical		
misery	miserable		
monotony	monotonous OPP. varied/interesting		
moral/morality	(im)moral		
notoriety	notorious		
pain	painful/painless		
power	powerful/powerless		
pride	proud		
region	regional		
relevance	(ir)relevant		

TABLE 4: Noun + adjective + verb

Noun	Adjective	Verb
ability	(un)able	to be able
acceptance	(un)acceptable	accept
adjustment	(un)adjustable	adjust
apology	apologetic	apologise
attraction	(un)attractive	attract
belief	(un)believable	believe
care	careful/careless	care (for sb./sthg.)
centre	central	centralise
conversion	convertible	convert
death	dead OPP. alive	die
decision	(in)decisive	decide
(in)dependence	(in)dependent / dependable	depend (on sb./sthg.)
difference	different OPP. same	differ
enjoyment	(un)enjoyable	enjoy
explanation	explanatory	explain (sthg. to sb.)
fertility	fertile OPP. barren	fertilise
harm	harmful/harmless / unharmed	harm
illness	ill OPP. well / fine	to be ill
imagination	(un)imaginative / imaginary	imagine
impression	(un)impressed / (un)impressive	impress
legality	(il)legal	legalise
life	living / alive OPP. dead	live
memory	memorable	memorise
mobility	mobile	mobilise / move
persuasion	persuasive	persuade
possession	possessive	possess
prediction	(un)predictable	predict
protection	protective	protect
reason	(un)reasonable	reason
recognition	(un)recognisable	recognise
reliability	(un)reliable	rely (on sb.)
resentment	resentful	resent
response	(un)responsive	respond
(dis)satisfaction	(dis)satisfied / (un)satisfactory	satisfy
sensitivity	(in)sensitive	sense
sleep	sleeping / asleep OPP. awake	sleep
stability	(un)stable	stabilise
success	(un)successful	succeed (in)
thought	thoughtful/thoughtless	think
tolerance	(in)tolerant	tolerate
value	valuable	value
variety	varied / various / variable	vary

──────── | **TABLE 5: Noun + adjective + verb** | ────────────

The following words are part of a group which forms verbs by adding '-en' to the noun or adjective (see Unit 16 Exercise 3).

Noun	Adjective	Verb
breadth	broad	broaden
depth	deep	deepen
height	high / tall	heighten
length	long	lengthen
	loose	loosen
	sharp	sharpen
	straight	straighten
strength	strong	strengthen
thickness	thick	thicken
	tight	tighten
weakness	weak	weaken
width	wide	widen

──────── | **TABLE 6: Noun + verb + adjective** | ────────────

The following words form a group in which each word has two adjectives (with '-ed' and '-ing'). The past participle (-ed) expresses how we feel, and the present participle (-ing) describes the thing/person which made us feel like that, e.g.

I was very *bored* at the party because the party was very *boring*.
We were *frightened* when the dog growled; the dog was *frightening* when it barked.

Noun	Verb	Adjective
boredom	bore	bored / boring
confusion	confuse	confused / confusing
depression	depress	depressed / depressing
disappointment	disappoint	disappointed / disappointing
embarrassment	embarrass	embarrassed / embarrassing
excitement	excite	excited / exciting
exhaustion	exhaust	exhausted / exhausting
fascination	fascinate	fascinated / fascinating
fright	frighten	frightened / frightening
frustration	frustrate	frustrated/frustrating
irritation	irritate	irritated/irritating
puzzle	puzzle	puzzled/puzzling
shock	shock	shocked/shocking
surprise	surprise	surprised / surprising
tiredness	tire	tired / tiring

Acknowledgements

The authors and publishers are grateful to the authors, publishers and others who have given permission for the use of copyright material identified in the text. It has not been possible to identify the sources of all the material used and in such cases the publishers would welcome information from copyright owners.

Maggie Stocking for the photograph on p. 3; Longman for the extracts on pp. 4–5 from the *Longman Dictionary of Contemporary English* and the *Longman Active Study Dictionary of English*; Oxford University Press for the extracts on pp. 4–5 from the *Oxford Advanced Learner's Dictionary of Current English*; Collins ELT for the extracts on pp. 5 and 39–40 from the *Collins COBUILD English Language Dictionary*; Punch for the cartoons on pp. 7, 29 and 51; The Manor House, Castle Combe, for the photograph on p. 25; Syndication International Library for the photograph on p. 35; Mirror Group Newspapers for the articles on p. 36; Chronicle Features, San Francisco for the cartoons by Gary Larson in *The Far Side* on pp. 38 and 75; Norman Myers for the extract from 'The captive costs' on p. 46, which first appeared in *The Guardian*; World Wide Fund for Nature United Kingdom for the photographs on pp. 46 and 48 by Behram Kapadia; World Press Network Ltd for the article on p. 55; Solo Syndication and Literary Agency Ltd for the cartoon by Mahood on p. 56, which first appeared in the London *Daily Mail*; Donna Dawson for the article on p. 57; W.H. Allen and Columbus Books for the cartoons on pp. 66 and 80; Anything Left-Handed Ltd for the illustrations on p. 85; Charles Peattie and Russell Taylor for the Alex cartoon on p. 89, which first appeared in *The Independent* and subsequently in *Alex II Magnum Force*, published by Penguin, © Charles Peattie and Russell Taylor 1988; *The Observer* for the extract on p. 90; Topham Picture Library for the photographs on p. 91; Camera Press for the photographs on p. 94; Burleigh Magazines Ltd for the photographs on p. 99, which first appeared in *Traditional Homes*; Curtis Brown Group Ltd for the extracts on p. 103 from *Kes* by Barry Hines, © Barry Hines 1968; David Higham Associates Ltd for the extract on p. 103 from *Billy Liar* by Keith Waterhouse; William Heinemann Ltd and Viking Penguin Inc. for the extract on p. 103 from *A Suspension of Mercy* by Patricia Highsmith; W.H. Allen for the extract on p. 103 from *Saturday Night, Sunday Morning* by Alan Sillitoe; A.M. Heath and Weidenfeld & Nicolson Ltd for the extract on p. 103 from *The Country Girls* by Edna O'Brien.

Illustrations by Chris Evans, Keith Howard, Leslie Marshall, Chris Pavely, Clyde Pearson and Wenham Arts.
Book design by Peter Ducker, MSTD.

Summary of exercises

Unit	Exercises	Self-study activities
1 Studying vocabulary	1 Ways of grouping vocabulary 2 Defining/paraphrasing skills 3 Creating a vocabulary filing system 4 Information about dictionaries	1 Describing words, e.g. *hyphen, capital letter* 2 Topic grouping
2 Beginnings and endings: Affixation 1	1 Noun and adjective suffixes, e.g. *-tion, -able* 2 Verb prefix *re-* 3 Adjective suffixes: *-ful, -less*	1 *un-* v. *in-* 2 Personal learning strategies 3 Verb prefix *un-*
3 Words around the house	1 Verbs, e.g. *burn, scratch* 2 Household objects: defining words 3 Garden vocabulary 4 Tools and gadgets: describing functions	1 Individual learning task 2 Topic grouping 3 Topic grouping
4 Finding partners for words: Collocation	1 Adjective + noun, e.g. *close friend* 2 Fixed phrases, e.g. *peace and quiet* 3 Topic chains 4 Adjective + noun, e.g. *rough sea*	1 Vocabulary storage 2 Personal learning strategies 3 Verb + noun, e.g. *make a mistake*
5 Travelling can be fun??	1 Clothes / personal belongings 2 Using words for emphasis, e.g. *even (bigger)*; describing a holiday 3 Travel phrases, e.g. *stay overnight* 4 Describing a holiday; travel brochure	1 Holiday problems 2 Words often confused 3 Extended writing 4 Different uses of *by*
6 Revision and expansion	1 Household objects 2 Verb + noun collocation 3 Pronunciation; silent letters 4 Listening 5 Situational phrases 6 Extended writing 7 Synonyms/antonyms	8 Suffixes 9 Collocation 10 Vocabulary game 11 Topic grouping 12 Meanings and collocation of common verbs 13 Ways of organising vocabulary

Unit	Exercises	Self-study activities
7 Money and finance	1 Banking vocabulary 2 Common mistakes, e.g. *lend* v. *borrow* 3 Financial vocabulary 4 Money and shopping	1 Words often confused, e.g. *bill* v. *fare* 2 Verb + noun collocation, e.g. *waste money* 3 Verbs + *up* and *down*
8 Connecting words and ideas 1	1 Expressing attitudes with adverbials, e.g. *to my surprise* 2 Using synonyms to structure text 3 Predicting topic vocabulary: accidents	1 Individual learning task 2 Extended writing 3 Synonyms
9 Communicating with people	1 Communication problems 2 Use of *thing(s)* 3 Words often confused, e.g. *argument* v. *discussion* 4 Colloquial language in a letter and cassette letter: guessing words in context	1 Verbs, e.g. *whisper* 2 Extended writing 3 Personal learning strategies
10 One + one = three: Compounds	1 Creative compound building 2 Car vocabulary 3 Leisure activities 4 Vocabulary game; compound building	1 Personal learning strategies 2 Creative compound building
11 Man and nature	1 Preserving rare animals: predicting vocabulary in a text 2 Types of animal; common adjectives 3 Animals in the wild; homophones	1 Word building 2 Personal learning strategies 3 Individual learning task
12 Revision and expansion	1 Compound words 5 Listening 9 Starting a car 2 Synonyms 6 Adjectives 10 Discussion 3 Pronunciation 7 Prepositions 11 Homophones 4 Situational dialogues 8 Accident network 12 Quiz	
13 Looking after yourself	1 Illnesses and symptoms: guessing words in context 2 Describing an illness 3 Phobias: guessing words in context 4 Food and health	1 Vocabulary storage 2 Borrowed words, e.g. *chef* 3 Personal learning strategies

»→

Unit		Exercises	Self-study activities
14	**Multi-word units**	1 Prepositional phrases 2 Miscellaneous phrases, e.g. *on the whole, what a shame* 3 Prepositional phrases 4 Phrasal verbs with *off*	1 Personal learning strategies 2 Phrasal verbs with *on*
15	**Work**	1 Jobs and duties 2 Work vocabulary, e.g. *career prospects* 3 Talking about one's job: guessing words in context 4 Factors in job satisfaction	1 Dictionary use 2 Vocabulary building and storage
16	**Affixation 2**	1 Adjective suffixes, e.g. *-al*; verb suffix *-ise* 2 Verb prefixes, e.g. *mis-* 3 Verb suffix *-en* 4 Noun suffix *-er*; adjective suffixes, e.g. *-ish*	1 Word building 2 Verb + noun, e.g. *a run, to run* 3 Prefix *dis-*
17	**Behaviour: People and verbs**	1 Common mistakes, e.g. *say* v. *tell* 2 Expressing probability; talking about relationships 3 Verbs and verb patterns, e.g. *manage* + inf. 4 Building stories with verbs	1 Verb patterns, e.g. verb + obj. + inf. 2 Phrases with common verbs, e.g. *make sense*
18	**Revision and expansion**	1 Phrasal verbs 2 Organising topic groupings 3 Word stress; word building 4 Food vocabulary 5 Suffixes 6 Listening	7 Dialogue building 8 Prepositions 9 Expressing probability 10 Prefixes 11 Sentence transformations
19	**Right v. left**	1 Different meanings of *right* 2 Left brain v. right brain 3 The problems of being left-handed 4 Left wing/right wing: political vocabulary	1 Antonyms 2 Vocabulary storage 3 Abbreviations
20	**Ways of looking at things**	1 Everyday objects 2 Unusual uses for everyday objects 3 Describing people: *look* + adj.; *look like* + noun; *look as if* . . .	1 Sense verbs, e.g. *taste* 2 Individual learning task 3 Things you look through, e.g. *microscope*

Unit	Exercises	Self-study activities
21 Problems	1 What you can do with a problem, e.g. *solve it, anticipate it* 2 Disasters: famine, earthquakes, pollution 3 Crime vocabulary 4 Bad habits, e.g. *dropping litter*	1 Word building 2 Extended writing 3 Describing problems, e.g. *it won't start*
22 Connecting words and ideas 2	1 Gradable/extreme adjectives 2 Link words 3 Modernising a house: antonyms in context	1 Individual learning task 2 Practice with link words 3 Topic grouping
23 Night and day	1 Phrases with *night* and *day* 2 Sleep vocabulary 3 Problems of working at night 4 Describing different times of day: guessing words in context	1 Defining and paraphrasing 2 Word building 3 Different uses of *at*
24 Revision and expansion	1 Describing and defining 2 Crime vocabulary 3 Connecting words and sounds 4 Link words 5 Word stress; word building	6 Identifying objects 7 Listening 8 Adjectives and adverbs 9 Extended writing 10 Professions